The
Story of the
COMMONWEALTH

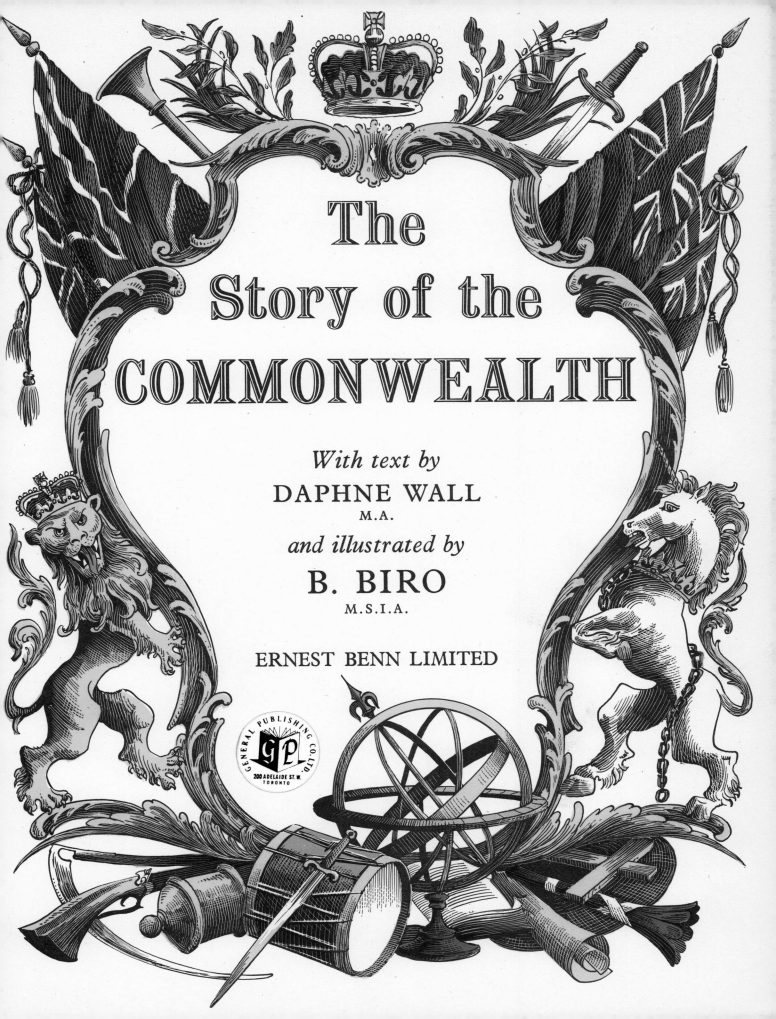

The Story of the COMMONWEALTH

With text by
DAPHNE WALL
M.A.

and illustrated by
B. BIRO
M.S.I.A.

ERNEST BENN LIMITED

GENERAL PUBLISHING CO. LTD.
200 ADELAIDE ST. W.
TORONTO

First published 1958
by Ernest Benn Limited at
Bouverie House · Fleet Street · London · E.C.4

© Ernest Benn Limited 1958

Printed in Great Britain

A THOUSAND YEARS ago men in Europe little dreamed of the true size of the world. They did not know that a huge continent, America, existed in the Atlantic Ocean, that even farther away across the Pacific lay Australia, that thousands of miles of tropical jungle were yet to be explored in Africa, and that there were ancient, mysterious countries such as India in the East. All these and many other lands have been charted and mapped today, and one-quarter of them, with one-quarter of the people living in the world, have come to belong together to the Commonwealth of Nations. The Commonwealth grew from the Empire that Britain, many hundreds of years ago, began to build up overseas. Ten independent countries belong to it today—Australia, Britain, Canada, Ceylon, Ghana, India, Malaya, New Zealand, Pakistan, and South Africa—together with many British dependencies. And since a thousand years ago many of them had not been discovered, the story of their association begins on the high seas, in small sailing ships, sailing out towards the unknown.

The first ships to cross the Atlantic from Europe were long and narrow. With only one square sail to catch the wind, they were rowed by tall, blond, fierce-looking sea-pirates from Scandinavia. The Vikings landed on the coasts of what is now Canada and, when they returned to Europe, they put their exploits into songs, which were handed down from father to son. Perhaps it was from the Vikings, who also invaded England, that the English gained their love of the sea. It was several hundreds of years before anyone else dared to follow where the Vikings had sailed, for mariners knew little of the art of navigation and did not dare to venture far from the coasts they knew. Then a Prince of Portugal, Henry the Navigator, made great improvements in sailing knowledge when he opened a School of Navigation, and in the fifteenth century a new spirit of daring and eagerness to find out more about the world swept over Europe. Great explorers, especially from Spain and Portugal, sailed farther and farther round the coasts of Africa, until they reached India by sea. Christopher Columbus was the first man since the long-forgotten Vikings to cross the Atlantic; and in 1497 John Cabot 'of kindly wit and a most expert mariner' set out from England on a voyage of exploration.

Cabot sailed on a northerly course and landed on the shores of Canada. When he returned he told his eager listeners that the land he had discovered was 'excellent and temperate and swarming with fish'. At first people thought that the American continent was 'the other side' of India or China, but they later realised that in fact they had stumbled on a whole New World. Spain found fabulous gold and silver mines in South America, and quickly built up a rich and powerful Empire there. England was slow at first to take part in these explorations and stake a claim in the New World, for she was much weaker than Spain and her navy was small; but a change was soon to take place.

5

Adventures and riches were beckoning in the New World, and no country could hope to have them without fine ships and the sailors to sail them. Henry VIII, the burly king who had six wives, realised this and began to build up England's navy; but it was in the reign of his daughter, Queen Elizabeth I, that English ships swept the seas, sailed round the world and defeated even mighty Spain.

'How cleverly that woman manages in everything', a foreign ambassador once said about the Queen. Although she loved to wear gorgeous dresses and fine jewellery, and to flirt with her courtiers, she certainly did manage to rule England extraordinarily well. Queen Elizabeth was tall, majestic, with pale, reddish hair, a long thin nose and dark, shrewd eyes. She could be very difficult if she chose, and often tried people's patience by constantly changing her mind, especially when she was fighting a battle of wits with the statesmen of other countries. Yet even when she grew old and bad-tempered, so strong and fascinating was her character that her subjects adored her, and she, too, loved them. 'I count this the glory of my crown, that I have reigned with your loves,' she said.

None served her more loyally than her sea-dogs, the many famous naval captains and admirals who built up England's sea-power in her reign. The Queen had mariners' charts hung in her room and took a great interest in all their voyages, even when her more staid counsellors disapproved. For it must be confessed that many of the sea-dogs were not over-scrupulous about boarding a richly laden ship and helping themselves to plunder—especially if that ship happened to be Spanish.

6

Most of the sea-dogs came from the West of England, and sailed on their adventures from the ports of Plymouth or Bristol. Such were the Hawkins family of shipowners. John and Richard Hawkins, father and son, fought side by side at sea. Brave sailor though he was, John Hawkins also made a fortune selling Negro slaves to the Spanish colonists in the New World, a traffic which men did not think to be as dreadful as we do today. On one journey, Hawkins's ships were caught in a gale and he entered a Spanish harbour in South America. The Spaniards received him as a friend, but then set fire to his ships. Hawkins only just managed to escape with his life. This treachery was not forgiven lightly by the sea-dogs, and was avenged by one who had escaped with Hawkins, and who became the greatest of them all—Sir Francis Drake.

Drake started life as an ordinary seaman and became the terror of the Spaniards, who called him 'The Dragon', although he did not look terrifying, being short and somewhat stocky with a sandy beard and a kind face. Drake sailed to Panama, captured a rich city and held up a mule train bringing treasure from Peru. He marched inland and climbed a great tree with notched steps cut into it and from the top he saw on one horizon the distant Atlantic and on the other the gleaming blue Pacific. He was the first Englishman to set eyes on the Pacific, and vowed to sail an English ship on those waters. He kept his vow. In his ship the *Golden Hind* he sailed from the tip of South America right up the Pacific coast as far as what is today San Francisco, and even farther, everywhere taking the Spaniards by surprise and loading his ships with treasure. Then he decided that instead of returning the way he had come he would strike out across the Pacific; so when he reached Plymouth after a two-year voyage, he had sailed triumphantly round the world —the second man and the first Englishman to do so.

The Spaniards were furious, but the Queen delighted; instead of cutting off Drake's head, as they wanted, she summoned him to London, went on board the *Golden Hind*, and knighted him with a golden sword.

Hawkins, Davis, Frobisher, Grenville, Drake—these and many other sea-dogs all fought together against the great Armada of ships which Spain sent to invade England. Drake was playing bowls when he was told the Armada had been sighted. 'There is time to finish the game and beat the Spaniards afterwards,' he said calmly. His confidence was justified when the English warships beat the Spanish galleons soundly and put them to flight for the last time, making England mistress of the seas.

A few years later took place one of the last and most famous sea-battles of Elizabeth's reign. Sir Richard Grenville in the *Revenge* was surrounded and attacked by fifty-three Spanish war-vessels. For fifteen hours Grenville resisted, until he had only sixty men left out of a crew of 250. Mortally wounded, he told his gunner to sink the ship, 'sink her, split her in twain,' rather than let her fall into enemy hands. Sir Richard Grenville was taken on board the Spanish flagship and there died, honoured even by his adversaries for his great courage.

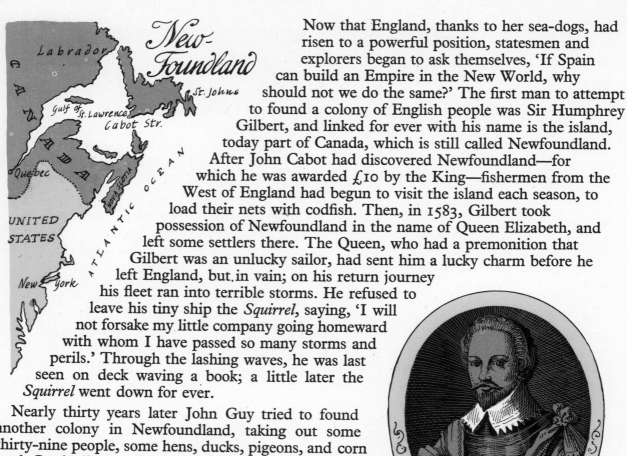

New-Foundland

Now that England, thanks to her sea-dogs, had risen to a powerful position, statesmen and explorers began to ask themselves, 'If Spain can build an Empire in the New World, why should not we do the same?' The first man to attempt to found a colony of English people was Sir Humphrey Gilbert, and linked for ever with his name is the island, today part of Canada, which is still called Newfoundland. After John Cabot had discovered Newfoundland—for which he was awarded £10 by the King—fishermen from the West of England had begun to visit the island each season, to load their nets with codfish. Then, in 1583, Gilbert took possession of Newfoundland in the name of Queen Elizabeth, and left some settlers there. The Queen, who had a premonition that Gilbert was an unlucky sailor, had sent him a lucky charm before he left England, but in vain; on his return journey his fleet ran into terrible storms. He refused to leave his tiny ship the *Squirrel*, saying, 'I will not forsake my little company going homeward with whom I have passed so many storms and perils.' Through the lashing waves, he was last seen on deck waving a book; a little later the *Squirrel* went down for ever.

Nearly thirty years later John Guy tried to found another colony in Newfoundland, taking out some thirty-nine people, some hens, ducks, pigeons, and corn seed. Gradually, too, fishermen from the West of England moved to Newfoundland to carry on their trade there. Fishermen from other countries also claimed the right to fish in the waters round Newfoundland, and a strange way of governing them all grew up. The master of the first ship to enter harbour in the spring was called Admiral of the Port, and dispensed rough justice for the season. It was not until the eighteenth century that their rule was brought to an end and Newfoundland governed as a normal British colony.

France made several attempts to capture Newfoundland, for she and England were rivals in North America. They attacked St. John's in 1696 and burned the town. They again tried to capture the town during the Seven Years War, and later still, during the time of Napoleon, made another attack on the island. France and England finally settled their differences over Newfoundland fishing rights by treaty. Newfoundland, still today an island of hardy sea-faring people, remained separate from Canada until 1949, when, having decided by vote to join Canada, she became the 10th province.

8

After Sir Humphrey Gilbert had been drowned, his handsome step-brother, Sir Walter Raleigh, enthusiastically took up his plans to found a colony in the New World, and obtaining a Charter from Queen Elizabeth, who loved him for his wit and gallantry, he sent out two ships to Virginia. These first colonisers, however, soon grew homesick, and returned to England. A second party sent out by Raleigh died at the hands of the Indians, and a third completely disappeared, leaving only the mysterious letters C R O cut on a tree. It seemed as if all Raleigh's efforts were doomed, but he refused to give up hope of Virginia. 'I shall yet live to see it an English nation,' he said. It was Raleigh who popularised the strange Indian custom of smoking; he smoked a silver pipe, and not even the bucket of cold water his servant threw over him, thinking he was on fire, could dampen his delight in tobacco.

In his later life, misfortunes crowded on Raleigh. In spite of all he did for his country, not only as a coloniser but as a scholar and poet, he was imprisoned for thirteen years in the Tower of London by King James, Queen Elizabeth's successor, who hated him. At last James released Raleigh to command an expedition to the 'large and bewtiful Empire of Guiana', thinking he would bring back gold. Raleigh reached and explored the country in South America which has since become British Guiana, a colony in the Commonwealth; but on his return, the King treacherously ordered his execution. As Raleigh knelt on the scaffold, he was asked if he wanted to face the east, and answered, 'So the heart be right, it is no matter which way the head lieth'. The crowd groaned as his head fell, and someone called out, 'We have not such another head to cut off.' So died one of the last and greatest of Queen Elizabeth's subjects. While the unlucky Sir Walter Raleigh was passing long days imprisoned in the Tower of

London, a company of merchants had taken over his plans, and decided to make yet another attempt to found a colony in Virginia. In 1606 about a hundred adventurous men set out, and this time when they reached the American shores they sailed some way up the smooth waters of a river which they called the James, in honour of the King, and built a fort at a sheltered spot on its banks. The flowers, the plum trees, and the wild strawberries made them think they had reached a paradise, but this blissful state did not last very long; they were constantly in danger of being attacked and scalped by the Indians, they quarrelled amongst themselves, and were desperately short of food. In one year, 144 out of 197 settlers had died.

In fact, the colony of Jamestown would probably have failed, like the previous ones, if a young man called John Smith had not come to the fore, and made the colonists settle down to till the soil, plant crops, and build strong defences against Indian attack. John Smith knew how to deal with his gentlemen colonists who had never laboured before and were more interested in making money quickly by discovering gold. If any of them swore an oath because of the blisters on his hands from chopping wood, he had a can of water poured down his sleeve. Having already had an adventurous life before he came to Virginia—he was sold as a slave and escaped—John Smith fell into the hands of some fierce Indian braves and was brought before their Chief, but his life was saved by the pleading of the Chief's pretty daughter, Pocahontas, who was then eleven years old. Pocahontas a few years later married one of the settlers, and with him went to England, where, to the great excitement of the English, who had never seen a Red Indian before, she was presented to the King and Queen.

It was the husband of Pocahontas, John Rolfe, who first succeeded in growing and curing a crop of tobacco to suit the tastes of people living in Europe. This was a very important discovery for Virginians. Great plantations of tobacco were laid out, and Negro slaves brought from Africa to work in them; docks were built along rivers, and ships from London and Bristol regularly visited them, bringing supplies for the colonists and taking aboard the crops of tobacco, packed in hogsheads. The prosperity of Virginia was built on this flourishing trade which has lasted to this day.

When the colony of Virginia was three years old, preparations were made to send out more colonists, and in the early summer of 1609 a brave fleet of nine ships sailed out of Plymouth Harbour. The fleet had sailed close together for six weeks, when a furious storm broke over them, and scattered the ships from each other. The flagship, the *Sea Adventure*, finding herself alone, sailed on through the storm for twenty-four hours when suddenly water rose five feet in the hold. The ship was leaking in many places, but the Governor, Sir George Somers, made the passengers stop up the leaks with meat and bail. He remained on deck for three days and three nights, but even he was beginning to despair, when a strip of land appeared on the horizon; it was the coral island of Bermuda.

The island was uninhabited, but the mariners when they landed did not go hungry, for wild pigs were running everywhere, and as Sir George Somers remarked, 'The Bermooda is the most plentiful place that ever I came to for fish, hogs and fowl.' They settled down happily and stayed for ten months, until they had built new ships in which they continued their voyage to Virginia. There, however, they found that the colonists were not nearly so well fed or happy as they themselves had been in Bermuda, and the following year many of them returned to the island with sixty more settlers. So in 1612, all because of a storm at sea, Bermuda became an English colony. The colonists built themselves wooden houses and cultivated the land. The ancient town of St. George grew up, and there, in 1620, gathered the first General Assembly, which is one of the oldest Parliaments, outside Britain, in the Commonwealth.

The clear seas and bays are perfect for sailing, as the colonists early discovered, for they became expert yachtsmen and shipbuilders. Yachting, swimming, spear-fishing, and sun-bathing are some of the pleasures which draw tourists to Bermuda every year, to spend their holidays on the island whose story inspired William Shakespeare to write his play *The Tempest*.

St. Peter's Bermuda

A few years after the American colony of Virginia had been founded, a group of English people who, because their Puritan faith was not tolerated in England, had decided that they, too, would emigrate, set sail from Plymouth in the *Mayflower*. They landed in country north of Virginia, still called New England, and set about building defences against the Indians and planting crops. By the autumn of that year they were able to gather their first harvest in the New World, which they celebrated with a feast of roast venison, wild duck, clams, cornbread, and wine from wild grapes. Side by side with Virginia and the Pilgrim Fathers' colony of Massachusetts, other colonies of English people grew up, each with its own character, according to the religion of its founders. The early history of all the American colonies is full of terrible battles fought between the white men and Indian braves with red-painted faces and feather head-dresses. Many settlers were killed and scalped, and the Indian, on his side, was gradually driven back from his lands, and today only survives in small numbers mainly on the western side of the American continent.

In 150 years from the first founding of Virginia, altogether thirteen colonies had grown up, from tiny weak settlements to strong, prosperous communities of independent people. Although Britain granted them freedom in many ways, she levied taxes on the colonists which, as they had no representatives in the government that imposed them, were bitterly resented. Their cry of 'No taxation without representation' eventually led to all the taxes being withdrawn, except one on tea. This caused more trouble than the rest put together. When three shiploads of tea arrived in Boston harbour in 1773, a band of colonists, disguised as Indians, rushed on board, and flung 342 chests of tea into the sea. The gauntlet was thrown; soon America and England has plunged into a war, which many people on both sides of the Atlantic hated, for it seemed like a Civil War of Englishmen against Englishmen. The colonists won their fight, and in 1776 the thirteen colonies declared their independence and became the United States of America. Yet this loss marked the beginning of a second British Empire; for thousands of colonists still wanted to remain attached to Britain, and they packed their belongings and travelled north, there to take part in the building of what was to become the largest country in the Commonwealth — Canada.

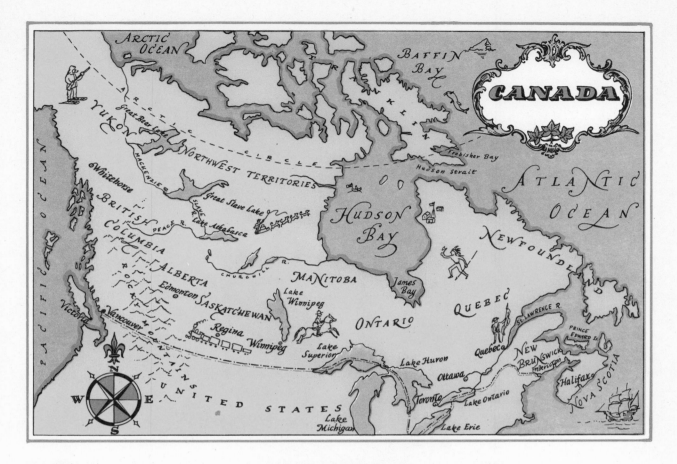

THE DREAM of finding the North-West Passage lured Englishmen in
Queen Elizabeth's time to push their little ships round Canada's northern
coast-lines into the ice-packs of the Arctic. In 1610, in a little ship called
the *Discovery*, sailed Henry Hudson, who had already discovered
the river on which New York now stands, and who longed to find the North Pole.
After many days at sea, Hudson reached the huge bay called after him. He and
his crew spent a miserable winter there, for their ship became frozen in. By the
spring, the crew were so desperate with hunger that they turned the great explorer
and his young son on to a small boat, and they were never heard of again.

Before this, French explorers had penetrated to the interior of Canada. In 1534
Jacques Cartier sailed up the great St. Lawrence River, making friends with the
Indians, who crowded round to see him wherever he went. He visited their
settlements on the sites of what are now the cities of Quebec and Montreal, and
bartered with the Indians for fur. As a result of Cartier's explorations, the French
and the Indians started a trade in fur, but it was not until many years later that
another Frenchman, Samuel de Champlain, set out to found a French colony in
the New World with 120 men. Champlain, noticing the spot where steep cliffs
rising on the banks of the St. Lawrence made a natural fortress, founded the city of
Quebec. Not only did he devote his whole life to building up the colony of New
France, but he also explored hundreds of miles of the Great Lakes by canoe,
and wrote a long book about the early history of New France, and the Indians' way
of life. The French were very concerned when they heard of the primitive society of
the Indians, and Jesuit missions went out to New France to convert them.

In the cold lands above the territories of New France on the St. Lawrence roamed buffalo, bear, deer, elk, and many other animals whose skins and furs were highly prized by Europeans. Above all, there was found the beaver, whose soft fur was used to trim fashionable hats and dresses. In search of this rich trade, the French settlers travelled ever farther into the interior of Canada, but now they began to meet English pioneers, in search of the same quarry; and so began a long rivalry. The English first started to take an interest in the fur trade of Canada when two French brothers-in-law, angry when the Government of New France confiscated some rich furs they had trapped, went to England instead of France to try to find support for a trading venture. They found their way to the court of Charles II, and there the King's cousin, Prince Rupert, listened fascinated to their tales of narrow escapes at the hands of the Indians, of hunting buffalo and bear, of shooting rapids, and of the beauty of the Canadian scenery. Prince Rupert determined to have a share in the fur trade, and became the first head of a 'Company of Adventurers of England trading into Hudson's Bay'. Under its Charter the company promised to carry out explorations as well as trade, to continue with the search for the North-West Passage, and to present the King of England—should he ever visit the company's domains—with the skins of 'two elks and two black beavers'. Not until 250 years after was the company called upon to honour this last promise; in 1939 King George VI visited Canada and was duly presented with two elk-skins and two beaver-skins.

The Hudson's Bay Company soon established itself. Trading posts sprang up along the rivers leading into Hudson's Bay, and there ships from England collected the furs and took them back to London, which soon rivalled France as a centre of the fur trade. Many of the early employees of the Hudson's Bay Company were hardy adventurers even more interested in exploring than fur-trapping. They pushed on westwards, covering thousands of miles by canoe, and meeting Indian tribes who had never seen white men before.

CHAMPLAIN

14

Meanwhile the rivalry between France and England in North America grew more and more serious, and in the middle of the eighteenth century, when France and England were at war in Europe as well, a final struggle decided the future of Canada. One of the most important battles in this war was the taking of Quebec In the spring of 1759, a fleet of forty warships and 100 transport ships arrived at the entrance of the St. Lawrence River with orders to take Quebec. Sending small boats ahead of them to chart the river, this fleet succeeded in sailing right up to Quebec, to the astonishment of the French. But now an even more difficult task lay ahead, for unless the citadel of Quebec could be captured before the winter came and froze

the river, the English would have to abandon their siege. In command of the besieging army was General James Wolfe, who had been specially chosen by William Pitt, the English minister, to take Quebec. But the summer wore on, attempts to storm the citadel failed, many men were sick, and Wolfe himself had fever, while the French general, Montcalm, kept watch night and day. The French, in fact, seemed impregnable, but Wolfe had noticed a point in the cliffs where women came down by a path to wash their clothes in the river. So, on a dark night, when the French were expecting some provisions, a small force under his leadership rowed to the foot of the path, tricked the sentry by answering his call in French, and clambered up the steep slope. When dawn broke, British redcoats were drawn up on the Plains of Abraham, and word was sent to Montcalm, who prepared for battle. The fighting was short but fierce. Wolfe, who was easily recognisable because of his great height, was mortally wounded and carried to the rear so that his men should not see him fall. Suddenly one of the officers with him cried 'They are running!' 'Who are running?' asked Wolfe. 'The French, sir.' 'God be praised,' said Wolfe, 'I can die in peace.' Montcalm fought with equal gallantry and he too died of his wounds.

15

After Wolfe's victory, the war between France and Britain was brought to an end, and France ceded to Britain all her colonies in North America. The British realised that the French-speaking Canadians would want to continue to practise their own religion and other customs, and they issued an Edict, granting them complete freedom to do so. This helped the French Canadians to come willingly into the British Empire and to live side by side with the English Canadians. The feeling that French and English belonged to one nation was soon put to the test when, in 1812, the newly created United States of America invaded Canada. French-Canadian and British soldiers fought side by side and successfully prevented the United States from encroaching on Canadian land.

At that time Upper Canada, Lower Canada, and the other British settlements were separate, and only formed part of the vast area which Canada occupies today. During the nineteenth century, she grew steadily in population by receiving thousands of immigrants from Britain, and in size through the discoveries of pioneers and explorers, who dreamed of extending Canadian territory 'from sea to sea'. In the north, the fur traders continued their conquests of new lands. Alexander Mackenzie, a young Scotsman, travelled in 1789 all the way down the river which is now called after him, but which he called the River of Disappointment, for, instead of leading him to the Pacific as he had hoped, it led him to the Arctic Ocean. But four years later he achieved his ambition by penetrating the Rockies and becoming the first man to cross Canada from east to west. Fraser and Thompson, two other explorers, also traced the course of some of Canada's rivers. The Pacific coast, once visited by Drake 200 years before, was explored by Captain Cook, who discovered part of Australia, and by Captain Vancouver, who gave his name to Vancouver Island.

Exploration went on in the Arctic, where sailors were still searching for the North-West Passage. An expedition led by Sir John Franklin at last proved that such a passage did exist, but it cost him his life, for he perished in the snow after abandoning his ice-bound ship.

In the wake of the pioneers and explorers, canals, roads, and railways were built. The first trans-Canada railway track of the Canadian Pacific Railway took five years to build, and nearly had to be abandoned several times when the promoters ran out of money; but at last, in 1885, the last spike of the track—a golden one—was driven in.

'Sir, it is my fervent aspiration and hope that some here tonight may live to see the day when the British American flag shall proudly wave from Labrador to Vancouver Island, and from Niagara to the Shores of Hudson's Bay.' A few years after George Brown, a Canadian Leader, had spoken these words, his prophecy came true: Upper Canada, Lower Canada, New Brunswick and Nova Scotia confederated to become, in 1867, the Dominion of Canada. When, in the next few years, Manitoba, British Columbia and the mighty North-west territories which had till then been ruled by the fur trading companies, joined the Federation, the new Dominion at last stretched 'from sea to sea'.

By this time important changes had taken place in Canada's government. There has been discontent at the form of her government, and some trouble, too, between French and English Canadians. So Britain had sent out the statesman Lord Durham to try to find a solution to Canada's problems. With a team of secretaries to help him, he had travelled all over Canada, collecting information, and then in 1839 he had issued a report, in which he had suggested that Canada should be granted a government which should be entirely responsible for its own affairs. This report was very important for up to that time the British Empire, like all the other Empires of the past, had been run on the principle that the Mother Country should have the last word on what the colony's government should or should not do. Lord Durham clearly saw that it would be much better for the colonies in the British Empire to change gradually from being dependent colonies to independent dominions. Canada was the first to do this; soon other colonies followed her example, and now there are ten fully independent members of the Commonweath. Nor has this Commonwealth development stopped, for the countries which are still dependent on Britain today are being taught to manage their own affairs, and will in the future themselves become members of the Commonwealth, quite independent of each other, but having the same kind of Parliament, with the Queen as the head of their association.

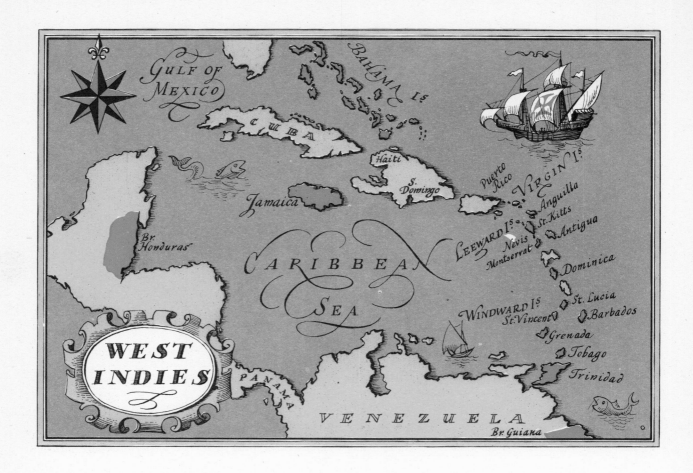

JUST A FEW years before John Cabot landed in Newfoundland, Christopher Columbus discovered, far to the south, the long sandy beaches, palm trees and blue skies of the West Indies. It seemed a miracle that he had crossed the Atlantic safely for the first time. Richly dressed, and bearing the royal banner of Spain, he went ashore, accompanied by the greater part of his crew, and there they knelt down on the beach of Watling Island in the Bahamas to give thanks for their arrival. From that day in 1492, Columbus spent twenty years on four long journeys, sailing farther south each time, and each time discovering more of the islands and coral reefs which stud the Caribbean Sea. But he never guessed he was on the fringes of a huge new continent unknown to Europeans. His aim had always been to find a westerly sea-route to India, and to the day he died he thought his islands were part of India—'the Indies'—and West Indies they are still called today.

Shy, brown-skinned men wearing head-dresses of feathers came to meet Columbus when he landed on Watling Island. They were the Arawaks. 'They carried no arms and did not know that a sword was sharp,' wrote Columbus. They were so gentle, in fact, they quickly died when the Spaniards tried to enslave them, and there are no Arawaks living now; but the hammock, which we are still using, was one of their inventions. The Caribs, another tribe in the West Indies, were much fiercer. When Europeans arrived to make their homes on the islands, they were often attacked by Caribs. The early settlers had a hard time in other ways too; food went bad in the hot climate, fevers were rife, and hurricanes sometimes whirled through the islands, destroying everything in their path.

18

But the settlers persevered, and began to bring slaves from Africa to do the hard manual work. French, Dutch and British followed the Spaniards out to the West Indies to found colonies. The first British settlement was little St. Christopher's Island, 'St. Kitts', and Barbados, Tobago, Antigua and Montserrat grew up in the next few years. The largest British island, Jamaica, was captured from the Spaniards for an odd reason. When Cromwell was ruling Britain he sent Admiral Penn and General Venables to take the Spanish colony of Hispaniola (the island that today forms the Dominican Republic and Haiti). The attack failed, so the two wily old men, afraid of Cromwell's wrath if they went back without a victory, captured Jamaica instead. It has been British ever since.

Great sea-battles were fought in the West Indies, and some of Britain's most famous admirals served here. One was Admiral Benbow, who, when his leg was shattered in battle with the French in 1701, directed the attack propped up in a chair. And then there was Admiral Rodney, who during the American War of Independence, in 1782,

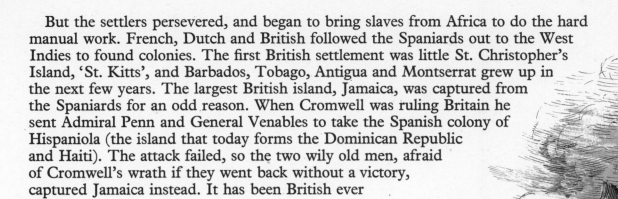

saved the British islands when France had captured most of them and was threatening the rest. 'The fate of the Empire is in your hands and I have no wish that it should be in any other's,' the Chief of the Admiralty told him. He was right, for at the 'Battle of the Saints', Rodney won a naval victory over the French. Seeing a gap in the enemy's line, he dashed through it, cutting their fleet into three parts which could not come to each other's aid. It was the first time this manœuvre had ever been executed in a naval battle. The battle was of exceptional importance since it not only saved Jamaica from a formidable attack, but after the disasters in North America helped to restore British prestige.

Two years later, Nelson himself was stationed in Antigua, when still a young naval captain. He fell in love—and got married in Fig Tree Church, Nevis. He came back to the West Indies a few years later as an admiral and chased the French fleet out of West Indian waters for the last time.

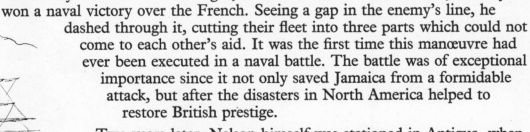

St HEN: MORGAN

The rival fleets of Britain, France and Spain did not provide the only seafaring men who have played an important part in West Indian history. A band of some of the most reckless, daring, swashbuckling pirates who have ever lived arose in the seventeenth century, and swarmed over the Caribbean seas with cutlasses and pistols at their belts, and two passions in their hearts—a hatred of the Spaniards and a greedy love for 'pieces of eight'. They were the Buccaneers, and their most famous leader was Henry Morgan. The incredible Captain Morgan took to the sea as a boy, and went to Jamaica with Penn and Venables; he joined the Buccaneers, and soon rose to be their admiral. At that time Jamaica was in danger of being attacked by the Spanish, and her Governor, Sir Thomas Modyford, decided he would rather have the Buccaneers as his friends than his enemies. So he came to an agreement with Morgan, that the Buccaneers should help to defend Jamaica, and, in return, they should be allowed to keep any loot from Spanish ships that might come their way.

Morgan sailed to Cuba and raided Puerto Principe, carrying off 500 oxen. Then he decided to attack one of the strongest cities in Panama. With only 400 men and no cannon, he overwhelmed three forts, looted the town and beat off a whole army. When the Governor of Panama wanted to know what wonderful weapons he had used, Morgan sent a pistol and a few bullets, with a message that if the Governor cared to keep them for a year, he would come back to fetch them. The Governor hastily sent a polite message and a present to Morgan, begging him not to trouble himself! Morgan and his men grew fabulously rich until at last Britain, who was trying to keep the peace with Spain, decided she must put a stop to buccaneering. Morgan was made the Governor of Jamaica, and this had the desired result. The old man set to work to suppress his former companions with almost as much gusto as he had once led them. Soon the Buccaneers were no more; but there must be a good many of their ghosts in the bays and creeks of the West Indies, and people are still hoping to find 'Morgan's Treasure', buried at the bottom of the Caribbean Sea.

20

Amidst these exciting times the colonists were busy learning what crops would grow best in the West Indies. At first they grew tobacco, but when this did not bring them enough money, they laid out huge plantations of sugar-cane. 'King Sugar' made them so rich that, by the eighteenth century, Columbus would hardly have recognised the West Indian scene. There were large, elegant houses on huge estates, and their owners were dressed in the latest fashions from London; there were carriages in the streets of the towns; and everywhere, working as servants in the great houses, cutting the sugar-cane in the fields and carrying it to the mills to be crushed, were negro slaves, some of them still longing for their home in Africa, and others, born in Jamaica, with no memory of any other home. Their conditions depended on the kindness or cruelty of their masters, who could buy, sell and punish them as they liked.

In Jamaica, in the wild hilly country in the centre of the island, lived also the Maroons—Negroes descended from the slaves of the Spaniards who had ruled Jamaica 200 years before, and who had set them free when they were driven out by the British. The Maroons were proud, wild and fierce, and when their leader, Cudjoe, led them in an uprising, the whole of Jamaica was terrified. The Maroons called on the slaves to join their numbers, but not as many came to their side as they wished, and after some fierce fighting they had to make peace. In return for laying down their arms the Maroons were allowed to return to live in freedom in the hills, and there their descendants are living today, with their own leader and individual way of life.

For over two hundred years the slave-trade went on without respite, and few people seem to have troubled themselves over the slaves' conditions. But in the eighteenth century opinion began to change. One day in 1765, Granville Sharp, the son of an English clergyman, was walking in Mincing Lane, London, when he noticed a runaway Negro slave who was sick and starving. Sharp rescued and nursed the slave, who had come from Jamaica. Two years later, when the slave was strong again, his old master claimed him back, but Sharp once more came to his rescue, and used his influence with the Lord Mayor of London to have him set free. From then on, he determined to fight for the freedom of all slaves.

Sharp fought a legal case with a man who had imprisoned a runaway slave in a ship on the river Thames. The Judge, after much deliberation, ruled that 'the air of England is too pure for a slave to breathe; let him go free', which meant that any runaway slave from the West Indies who managed to reach England became by law a free man. Sharp found an ally in Thomas Clarkson, who, when a student at Cambridge, wrote an essay on slavery, and then decided to devote his whole life to the cause of abolition. Clarkson visited slave ships to see conditions with his own eyes, and toured the country, stirring up public opinion. The slave-traders, of course, hated him, and a gang of men once nearly killed him by trying to push him off a pier into the sea. But he was not easily frightened.

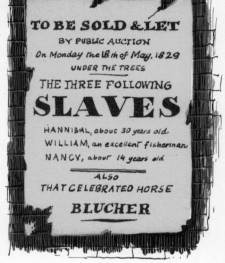

The man who fought for the cause of slavery abolition in Parliament was William Wilberforce. Year after year he made eloquent speeches in the House of Commons, with the support of three other great statesmen of the time— Pitt, Fox and Burke. At last, in 1807, their efforts were crowned with success, and the slave-trade was abolished. Those at present under slavery had still to be freed, and this was done in 1833, when the Government announced it would pay twenty million pounds compensation to the slave-owners. Wilberforce, by now an old man, died four days after hearing that his life's work had been completed. And the night before the Bill became Law, hundreds of slaves in the West Indies climbed the hills to see the dawn of their first day of freedom.

WILBERFORCE

The end of slavery in the West Indies, welcome though it was, brought problems both to the workers and to their former masters. In some islands, the transition to freedom went quite smoothly, and the former slaves stayed on their old plantations as freemen, receiving wages. But in Jamaica and other islands, the one-time slaves left the plantations to cultivate their own ground, and the planters found it difficult to manage the sugar estates without them. When, as a final blow, the price of sugar fell in Britain, many of the planters were ruined, and once magnificent houses and estates fell into decay. As it was on sugar that the islands depended, everyone suffered.

Other disasters overtook the West Indies; Antigua had a severe earthquake, Jamaica several years of drought, and there were epidemics of disease. Gradually, however, better times came to the islands. New crops were planted such as coffee, bananas and oranges, while special ships on which fruits could ripen slowly without becoming rotten helped West Indians to export them. Gradually, too, the West Indians whose ancestors had once been so disunited—planters on one hand, slaves on the other—grew into one people. And this was no small achievement considering that many races—Negro, European, and even Chinese—have blended together in the West Indies. Different though the West Indians may be in their ancestry, they have developed a character which is all their own. They are great cricketers; wherever you go in the West Indies you will hear talk of the latest Test Match score; you will hear, too, plenty of laughter, for West Indians are gay and light-hearted; and you will hear, of course, the singing of the calypsos.

Recently the West Indies drew closer together, by forming a Federation, which has its Parliament in Trinidad. In this way, the different colonies are making themselves into one strong, united state in order to take their place as an independent member of the Commonwealth.

23

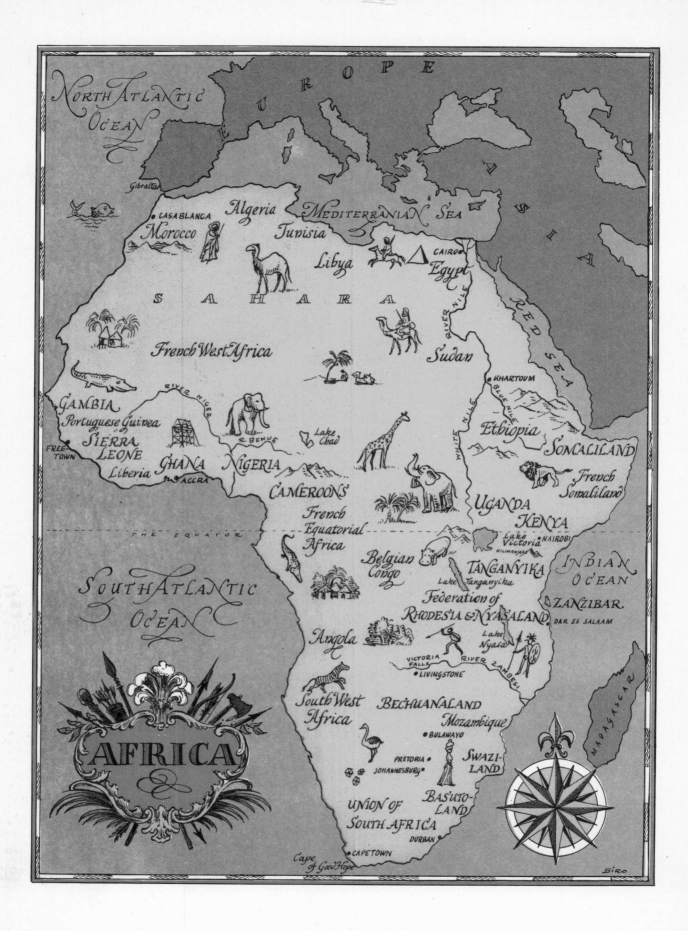

THE MIGHTY continent of Africa was explored far later than America. All but its coast-line was still a mystery less than a hundred years ago, and it was known as the 'Dark Continent'. The early explorers found much to wonder at: witch doctors with strange powers of magic; hundreds of different tribes, some with ancient civilisations, others so primitive that they did not know the use of the wheel; great lakes, jungles and mangrove swamps, mountains and deserts; and every variety of wild life. No wonder Africa fascinated early travellers, so that many of them lost their lives in its exploration.

Most of Africa's present boundaries were also created less than a hundred years ago, by European countries, who competed with one another for a claim in Africa, and finally agreed at a conference to divide it into 'spheres of influence'. The areas where British pioneers had been most active became part of the British Empire, and today eight countries—six dependencies and two independent members, Ghana and South Africa—belong to the Commonwealth.

It was West Africa which first came into contact with Europeans. About the time of the discovery of the New World, Portuguese and British sailors landed on the surf-pounded beaches and met Africans wearing 'collars and bracelets, hoopes and chaines of gold, copper and ivory'. They began to trade in these wares, and the trading forts

built by the Europeans laid the foundations of the future British colonies of Sierra Leone, the Gambia, the Gold Coast and Nigeria. The traders were not satisfied with gold and ivory for long. As you know from the story of the West Indies, they started to buy slaves. The unlucky Africans were seized by stronger tribes, tied together with thongs, and made to march hundreds of miles to the coast. Many of them died on the way. Years later, however, when the slave-trade was abolished, the British Navy patrolled the coasts of West Africa, and rescued thousands of slaves. To provide new homes for these rescued slaves some of the men who were fighting the slave-trade in Britain bought land in Africa for them; and that is how the colony of Sierra Leone began, whose capital city today tells its story by its name—Freetown.

During the hey-day of slavery, a mighty Empire was built up in the interior of West Africa by a tribe called the Ashanti. The legend says that a magician came to the court of Osai Tutu and told him that he must make the Ashanti a great nation. The magician drew down a black cloud from the sky out of which came a Golden Stool. 'This Golden Stool,' said the magician, 'contains the soul of the Ashanti people.' The Stool, which has its own State Umbrella, has been guarded carefully by the Ashanti people, who today form part of Ghana.

25

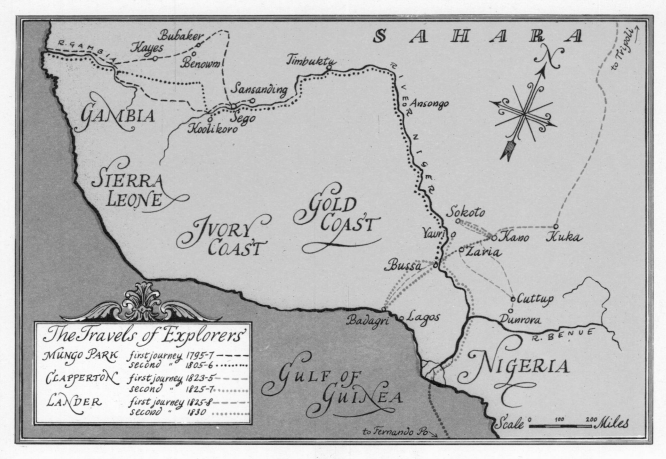

The Travels of Explorers

MUNGO PARK first journey 1795-7 ----
second " 1805-6 ....

CLAPPERTON first journey 1823-5 — —
second " 1825-7 ....

LANDER first journey 1825-8 ---
second " 1830

It was tantalising for those who knew the coast of West Africa to be ignorant of the interior. Explorers were especially curious about the fabulous city of Timbuktu, of which the Arabs said the houses were roofed with pure gold, and of the true course of the great river Niger, which for hundreds of years was thought to flow westward straight across Africa. So an association was formed in 1788 to promote exploration in Africa, and it sent out a young Scotsman, Mungo Park, to explore the Niger.

Wearing strange clothes for an explorer—a blue coat with gilt buttons, and a tall, beaver hat—Mungo Park set out from the river Gambia with six attendants, a 'few changes of linen, an umbrella, a pocket sextant, a magnetic compass, and a thermometer'. He travelled through Negro and Moorish kingdoms, and met with many adventures, being teased about his long nose, red beard and skin, which, said some Africans, was white because his mother had dipped him in milk as a child. Just as he was beginning to think he was near the golden dream of reaching the Niger, Mungo Park was captured by a party of Moors. He was ill-treated and made to drink the same water as the cattle, but he managed to escape on his horse. After many more hardships, he caught sight of the 'long-sought-for Niger, glittering in the morning sun', and to his great joy, it was, as he had set out to prove, flowing eastwards. Mungo Park returned to Britain, married and settled down, but the lure of Africa was strong, and he returned on another expedition.

He took a large party with him this time, but they met with so many misfortunes, from attacks by hostile tribes to being scattered by a huge swarm of bees, that by the time they reached the Niger only a few were still alive. Mungo Park started to sail down the Niger in a canoe, but he never returned; his friends learned later that he was drowned while crossing some dangerous rapids.

Many other explorers continued Mungo Park's work. A party travelled from North Africa across the scorching Sahara desert, seeing in the south the skeletons of slaves who had died on their journeys to Arab countries. In this party was Clapperton, who later visited the King of the Hausa. When Clapperton died from fever, the servant who had nursed him, Richard Lander, finished the journey he had begun, and became a great explorer himself. He and his brother John travelled together and were captured by an Ibo Chief, who said he would not let them go until he received goods valued at 20 slaves. An African took pity on them and ransomed them, and they eventually reached home safely, having at last solved the mystery of the course of the Niger.

Another West African explorer was a demure lady who wore a long black silk dress, voluminous Victorian petticoats, and a little black bonnet, and did not see any reason to vary this attire even when she was on safari, sailing down swift rivers in canoes, or crossing swamps and marshes up to her neck in water. Mary Kingsley, gentle as she was, was afraid of nothing; not even of cannibals, with whom she traded her spare clothes when she found herself alone in their village; nor of a crocodile when it put its head over the edge of her canoe, and which she hit smartly on the nose; nor of a wild tiger which she once freed from a stake, firmly ordering it to 'Go home, you fool'. She contributed much to our knowledge of West Africa. 'My African friends have used me as a doctor, an artisan, a prophet, a charm against the smallpox and have had hopes of turning me into a general,' she wrote. She loved them and championed their cause, and when she died nursing in South Africa she was mourned in distant jungle villages as well as in her own country.

Missionaries followed the explorers out to West Africa, and set up hospitals and schools. The famous missionary James Aggrey did not have to go to Africa, however, for he was born in the Gold Coast just over eighty years ago, the son of a Fanti princess and the Ceremonial Spokesman of the Anamabu Paramount Chief. Aggrey went to a mission school and at the age of fifteen he himself became a schoolmaster of a little village school. He was only sixteen when he preached his first sermon, and soon began to travel all over Africa, and later went to England and America. Everywhere he went, people flocked to hear his sermons, which were full of wisdom, and yet so humorous that his audience sometimes held their sides with laughter.

'You can play a tune of sorts on the white keys,' said Aggrey, 'and you can play a tune of sorts on the black keys, but for harmony you must use both the black and the white.' He meant that the African and the white man must work together for the good of West Africa, and his words took root, for in the Gold Coast and the other colonies in West Africa, British administrators and Africans worked hard together to fight the many diseases which ravaged the country, to build roads and cities, and to improve crops. The most important crop to be developed in the Gold Coast was cocoa, for today it provides a great part of the country's livelihood; most of the chocolate we eat comes from West Africa's cocoa plants. In 1957 occurred a great day in the history of the Gold Coast. Like Canada and other British colonies many years ago, it was granted independence by Britain, and, with Dr. Nkrumah as its first Prime Minister, became yet another full member of the Commonwealth, under the new name of Ghana.

After the river Niger had been explored, British traders began to build posts along its forest-clad banks. A trading company was formed which was granted a Royal Charter, and gradually controlled much of the coast lands round the Niger. Far inland, in towns and cities of which even the huge arches and domes, walls and parapets, were made of elaborately patterned mud, lived tribes quite different from those in the south. They were Moslems, who dressed in flowing Arab robes and rode camels. Their rulers maintained ceremonial courts, but were often cruel and raided weaker tribes for slaves.

Into these regions the Royal Niger Company sent Captain Frederick Lugard, who was already famous for his work in East Africa, to negotiate treaties with the much-feared Kings of Borgu, from whose realms it was said no white man had ever returned alive. The French, who were extending their West African Empire, also dispatched a messenger with the same purpose, and it became a race of great importance as to who should reach the capital, Nikki, first. Lugard won, travelling with amazing speed, although he had never been in West Africa before. He duly made treaties of protection with the Borgu Kings, with many of whom he became friendly, and so the great country of Nigeria, as it is today, began to take shape. Lord Lugard, as he later became, worked tirelessly for many years to make Nigeria strong and peaceful, and when its different regions united in 1914, he became its first Governor-General. He managed to put a stop to slave-trading, the favourite pastime of the northern Emirs. But when they had been defeated in battle by Lugard they were as often as not, given back their thrones, for he had developed a system of government called 'Indirect Rule'. Under this system, which has since been followed in many other British colonies, the traditional chiefs or leaders continued to rule as they had always done, only supervised and helped by British District Officers.

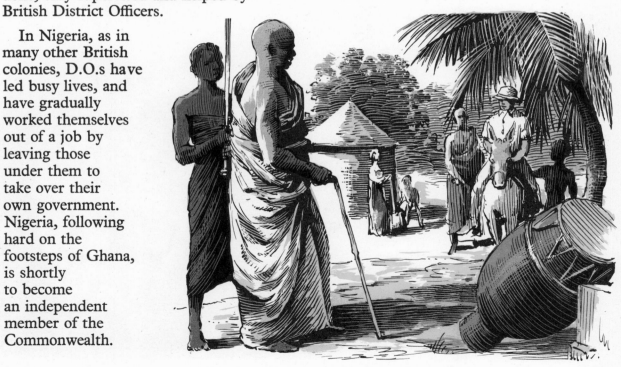

In Nigeria, as in many other British colonies, D.O.s have led busy lives, and have gradually worked themselves out of a job by leaving those under them to take over their own government. Nigeria, following hard on the footsteps of Ghana, is shortly to become an independent member of the Commonwealth.

LORD LUGARD

The whole continent of Africa from east to west was first crossed on foot by the great Scottish doctor, explorer and missionary David Livingstone, who made known huge areas of Central and East Africa on his long journeys. It was Livingstone who discovered Victoria Falls, called by the Africans 'the sounding smoke'; near the majestic roar of its waters chiefs offered prayers and sacrifices, and the more practical Livingstone planted a hundred peach and apricot stones. On other journeys Livingstone discovered the beautiful Lake Nyasa and the country around it which is now Nyasaland, part of the Commonwealth. It was here that Livingstone, who was deeply religious, became more and more horrified at what he learned of the Arab slave-trade, which he did all he could to suppress.

When no news was heard of Livingstone, an American newspaper sent out Henry Stanley to find him. With little idea of the explorer's whereabouts, Stanley succeeded in tracing Livingstone. Excited though the two men were to see each other, they did not show their feelings. Stanley took off his hat, and said, 'Dr. Livingstone, I presume?' Livingstone by this time was sick and old, but refused to return home with Stanley. Not long after he died, and his faithful servants Susi and Chummah travelled for nine months carrying the body of their beloved master to the coast. He was buried in Westminster Abbey.

Since the beginning of history the river Nile has been venerated, for it provides a huge portion of Africa with life-giving water; yet for centuries its source was unknown. Among the explorers who sought to solve this mystery were Burton and Speke. At first they travelled together, and discovered the great Lake Tanganyika. Burton was delighted with its beauty, but Speke, who had gone temporarily blind through sickness, observed sadly, 'The lovely Lake Tanganyika could be seen in all its glory by everybody but myself.' Later, however, Speke had the consolation of discovering by himself Africa's greatest lake, Victoria. He rightly decided it was the source of the Nile, but Burton did not agree with him, and the two explorers quarrelled over this for the rest of their lives.

Another of Africa's enormous and beautiful lakes was discovered by Samuel White Baker, whose wife went with him on his most dangerous journeys.

Speke was the first white man to visit the strange and ancient kingdom of Buganda, which now forms part of the British Protectorate of Uganda, and to meet its despotic King, Mtesa. When Mtesa wanted to test Speke's gun he thought nothing of having one of his subjects shot, and once he had the inhabitants of a whole village thrown into a lake because the witch doctor said it would cure the Queen's toothache. But Mtesa was also broad-minded and invited Christian missionaries to enter his kingdom. Many went

out, risking the hostility of Africans and of the Arab slave-traders. One missionary, Alexander Mackay, set up a printing press, and produced copies of the Gospel, which were in such demand that Africans read it sitting in a circle, so that a number learned to read upside down, and could not read any other way. As well as teaching the Gospel, the missionaries fought disease and slavery, but when Mwanga, Mtesa's son, succeeded to the throne he persecuted the missionaries and their converts, burning them or even feeding them to crocodiles. In 1885, Bishop Hannington who was attempting to find a new route to Uganda, was imprisoned under Mwanga's orders in a filthy hut, swarming with rats and vermin. After eight days his men were murdered and later he himself was speared to death by Mwanga's soldiers.

31

To help British explorers and missionaries in East Africa the Imperial East Africa Company was formed by Royal Charter, and in 1890 it sent out Frederick Lugard (who later served in Nigeria) to negotiate a treaty with Mwanga. The Company began to lose money, and decided to leave Uganda. Lugard was horrified, and he hurried back to England to persuade the Government to take over responsibility for the country. As a result, Britain assumed a Protectorate over Mwanga's kingdom, which was later extended until it included the whole area of Uganda as it is today. Thus, Buganda is part of Uganda, which may seem a little confusing—but not nearly as confusing as the fact that the people of Buganda are called Baganda, a single man is a Muganda, and the language he speaks Luganda.

'Where it will start from no one can guess, where it is going to nobody knows,' so ran a somewhat unkind poem about the railway through Uganda, which was begun a year after the creation of the Protectorate. The tremendous difficulties of building such a railway over swamps, dangerous tsetse fly country, dense bush, rock, ravines and swift rivers, earned it the name 'The Lunatic Line'. When the railway builders reached Tsavao, all work stopped because man-eating lions terrorised the camp and ate large numbers of the workers. The lions were finally shot, and the line went on. Its completion in 1903 helped Uganda to develop rapidly though she has kept to her ancient system of kingships. Half a century ago ivory was the country's only export, but today cotton, coffee, sugar, gold and groundnuts make their way down the line to the coast and to the world's markets.

The long lines of slaves who excited David Livingstone's pity as they wended their way through Africa would reach their journey's end in the huge slave-market of the island of Zanzibar off the East Coast of Africa. Small though the island is, its Arab Sultans once ruled a large part of East Africa. 'When you play the flute in Zanzibar, all Africa as far as the Lakes dances,' said an Arab proverb. The early explorers nearly always started their journeys inland from the town of Zanzibar, buying equipment and hiring porters in the narrow Oriental streets with their huge, intricately carved doorways. Britain eventually succeeded in persuading the Sultan of Zanzibar to abolish slavery in his domains, and gradually the Empire of Zanzibar was reduced to the island itself and a ten-mile strip of the coast. Today it is still ruled by its Sultan, and is a Protectorate within the Commonwealth.

The British colony of Kenya was once part of the Empire of Zanzibar. This was the land—much of it mountainous—through which the railway to Uganda was being built, and as it was running at a great loss, Britain decided to try to develop Kenya, and invited Europeans to settle on parts of Kenya not already inhabited by African tribes and build up farms. Many settlers from South Africa and Britain went to Kenya, and although they had great difficulties at first, their farms eventually began to prosper. Lord Delamere spent a huge fortune experimenting with sheep and cattle, and with wheat, to determine what type of farming was most suited to Kenya, and largely due to his work the colony of Kenya has now become a rich agricultural country. It was here that Princess Elizabeth, as she then was, while staying the night in 'Treetops', a little hotel built on top of a huge tree, heard that her father had died and that she was therefore Queen.

SOUTH AFRICA'S southernmost tip was called by the first sailors who rounded it in Columbus's day 'Cape of Storms', but soon renamed 'Cape of Good Hope', because it meant there was now good hope of reaching India by sea. Sailors in ships passing by gazed at the extraordinary mountain with a flat top like a table rising from the Cape, but if they landed it was not to stay long; they used it as a half-way house on their journeys to India, stopping only to fill their water flasks, leave their letters under a big stone to be collected by the next ship passing in the other direction, and sometimes to barter for cattle with the brown-skinned Hottentots, who had little tufts of hair sticking up on their heads. Only the Hottentots ventured to the coast to meet the white men, but farther inland lived Bushmen with poisoned blow-pipes, fierce Zulu warriors, and many other different African tribes.

In 1652 a party of Dutch settlers arrived to make their home in the Cape, and they built a flourishing colony whose capital was called Cape Town. Some of the settlers, however, abandoned town life, and became farmers. Seeking new lands in which to graze their cattle, they trekked inland in their covered ox-wagons, and for days on end their children would be rocked to sleep by the jolting of the huge wheels, until suitable country was found to build a farm. The Boers had to fight against Hottentots and Bushmen, who attacked them with darts and spears. They hunted their own food, taught their children themselves, for of course there were no schools, and since they could not go to church conducted their own services and Bible readings. This tough life gave them a special character. They developed their own language, Afrikaans (the name given to them— Boer—is Afrikaans for farmer). They were downright, simple folk, with a strict religious faith, dressed usually in blue cloth jackets and trousers, and very large hats. They liked their self-reliant life, and hated anything which might threaten to change it.

However, a change was coming to Cape Colony. When Britain and Holland were at war, the Prince of Orange fled to Britain and called on the Dutch colonies to place themselves under British protection. It was returned to Holland when peace was declared, but not long after, in Nelson's day, Britain captured the Cape, and this time kept it at the end of the war, paying Holland six million pounds.

Soon British settlers arrived in South Africa. The Boers resented their coming, for although some British farmed and helped, others became town-dwellers and did not understand the Boers' way of life. The Boers grew especially bitter when Britain abolished slavery throughout the Empire, for they had grown used to running their farms with slaves. So they decided to go farther away from the British and the town life they

34

despised, and in 1836 thousands of ox-wagons, piled high with furniture, belongings and food, started off on the longest trek of all, the 'Great Trek' into the unknown north. The journey was the most difficult the Boers ever made. Over mountains they had to take the wheels off their carts and let them slide like toboggans. In lowlands, there was danger from fever. Lions had to be warded off. And most dangerous of all were the African tribes, who were angry and afraid at the advance of the white man. One tribe, the Xhosas, believing that they were carrying out orders from the spirits of their dead, killed their own cattle and destroyed their crops, expecting a great hurricane to drive all white men into the sea on a certain day. When the day arrived and nothing happened, their spirit was broken and, despite all the efforts of the governor to save them, they began to die in thousands. The Zulus, on the other hand, fought implacably, and nearly forced the Boers to leave their new-found lands.

But in 1848 the Boers won a great victory over them at Blood River, and set up the republic of Natal. The British, however, considered that although the Boers had left British territory, they were still British subjects owing allegiance to the Crown, and five years later Natal became a Province of Cape Colony. It was not until opinion in Great Britain had turned in favour of the Boers that they were able to found two new States, the Transvaal and the Orange Free State.

PAUL KRUGER

Many of the Boers thought the British were responsible for the sufferings they endured in the Great Trek, and so began feelings of hatred which were to come to a head in a war. A little boy of twelve took part in the Great Trek, whose name was Paul Kruger, and who grew up to be leader of the Boers in their fight against the British.

The four South African states which had come into being—Cape Colony and Natal, the Orange Free State and Transvaal, were not at first rich countries; but thirty-two years after the Great Trek, something happened which changed their whole history. Some farmer's children, playing on the banks of the Orange River, found a pretty white pebble, and kept it as a toy. When a visiting farmer saw it he had it tested and found it was a diamond. Soon other diamonds were found on the banks of the Vaal, and in another stretch of land which later became the town of Kimberley. The exciting news spread like lightning, and from all over the world rushed thousands of people eager to make themselves millionaires—as indeed they had every chance of doing—provided their eyes were sharp as they burrowed in the soil, and shook it carefully through their fine sieves. The famous Cullinan Diamond was presented to Edward VII by the Transvaal Government. The largest of the nine 'Stars of Africa' into which it was cut is mounted in the Sovereign's Sceptre, which can be seen in the crown jewels at the Tower of London. This is the largest cut diamond in the world.

Only a few years later, news of a second discovery shook the world. This time it was gold, found in the Boer state of Transvaal. Again men in thousands poured to the spot where they thought they could make their fortune, travelling—for there were no railways—on bicycles, on mules, in carts or coaches, even in hansom cabs. The price of the farms through which ran the greatest goldreef in the world rocketed. The gold diggers lived in ox-wagons, tents and tin shanties; their motley, untidy camp became a town with a hundred thousand inhabitants in ten years, and where there were once mud huts there are now the shops, streets and skyscrapers of Johannesburg. The discovery of gold and diamonds turned South Africa into a rich country. But many of the Boers shook their heads disapprovingly. They did not like the foreign business men who came pouring into their land, and the new towns that were springing up everywhere. Even Paul Kruger, who had become President of the Transvaal, and knew his country needed the revenue gold could bring, prophesied that the newly found gold 'will cause our country to be soaked in blood'.

Into the bustling diamond camp at Kimberley arrived a young man called Cecil Rhodes, who had come from England not long before to improve his delicate health. In order to make enough money to study at Oxford, which was his great ambition, he bought a small steam-engine, and hired it out to pump flooded pits; and sometimes he used it to make ice-creams, in which he did a roaring trade with the hot and thirsty miners. Soon he was buying diamond mines himself. Then in a few years he took his Oxford degree, became a member of the Cape Colony Parliament, then Prime Minister; and all the time his diamond interests grew until he controlled the largest diamond market in the world and had become a millionaire.

Cecil Rhodes

Rhodes was not, however, interested in money for its own sake, but because it brought the power he needed to further his grand designs. These included nothing less than making Africa British from 'top to toe'—from the Cape to Cairo. It was Rhodes who persuaded the British Government to annex Bechuanaland, laying the foundations of the British Protectorate today. But most of his empire-building was carried out quite independently of the Government. Just as Raleigh had done before him, Rhodes applied for a Royal Charter. The British South Africa Company he formed added a huge new territory to the British Empire, called Rhodesia in honour of its founder, and years after Rhodes's death, Rhodesia joined with Nyassaland to make, today, the Federation of Rhodesia and Nyassaland, an almost fully independent country in the Commonwealth. Rhodes's name lives, too, in the scholarships he founded for young people from the Commonwealth and America to study in his beloved Oxford University. Although he has been much criticised for his policy before the outbreak of the Boer War, he was undoubtedly one of the greatest of the many great men who have helped build the empire.

Rhodes's great opponent was Paul Kruger, the President of the Transvaal. These two men, although alike in determination, fearlessness, and devotion to their country's interests, were different in most other ways. Rhodes believed in modern progress and big business. Kruger was conservative and old-fashioned. He did all he could to hamper the gold prospectors in Johannesburg; but the 'Uitlanders', as they were called—they were mostly British—

felt that they were being unfairly treated, especially as it was they who were making the Transvaal rich. This and many other quarrels caused by the opposing views of the British and the Boers: Rhodes—by now a sick man—determined to unite South Africa at almost any cost; Kruger equally fanatical in his determination to keep Transvaal for the Boers alone, resulted in war breaking out in 1899. Although the British thought that the war would be quickly finished by 'fifty thousand horse and foot going to Table Bay', for the first few months things went very much against them, and several of their towns were besieged. In charge of the defence of Mafeking was Lord Baden-Powell (the founder of the Boy Scout Movement). He held out bravely, and when at last Mafeking was relieved, there was wild rejoicing. Among the many other famous men who took part in the South

African war was the young Winston Churchill (as he then was), who was reporting the war for a London paper. Travelling in a train which ran into an ambush, he was captured by the Boers, but, undaunted, he later scaled his prison wall, and leapt on to a moving train; after hiding at the bottom of a mine, he finally regained the British frontier.

The war lasted for two and a half years, and involved what for those days were gigantic armies, nearly 400,000 men taking part in the fighting. Although the British succeeded in annexing the two Republics after eleven months, the Boers retired to their farms and became guerrilla fighters. There

38

were great generals on both sides—on the English, Lord Roberts and Lord Kitchener, and on the Afrikaner, Botha, De Wet, and Smuts. These three generals fought to the last moment, but gave in, in 1902, and peace was declared. By this time many farms and lands had been destroyed in hunting down the guerrilla fighters, so the first action of the British Government was to give three million pounds to help repair the damage. It also granted freedom to teach Dutch in schools, which laid the foundations of a South Africa developing freely as part Afrikaner-speaking and part English-speaking. The generous terms of peace helped to mend the old quarrels between the Afrikaner and British settlers, although there were still differences between them which have lasted to the present day.

The Boers were especially reconciled when Britain quickly granted full self-government to the colonies she had annexed. Six years after the end of the war all four colonies, which had only recently been bitterly fighting each other, met at a conference in Pretoria, and General Botha himself moved a resolution that 'the best interests and the permanent prosperity of South Africa can only be secured by an early Union, under the Crown of Great Britain, of the several self-governing colonies'. So the British Parliament passed in 1910 an Act by which the Union of South Africa came into being. And when the war against Germany broke out in 1914, it was Afrikaner troops under Britain's old enemy, General Botha, who helped Britain by invading German South-west Africa; and General Smuts drove the Germans out of German East Africa. Smuts went to England and joined the Imperial War Cabinet; he became a great international statesman, helping to found the League of Nations. Later on when he returned to South Africa and became Prime Minister, King George VI visited South Africa with his family and saw much of the country's farms, mines, cities and magnificent scenery.

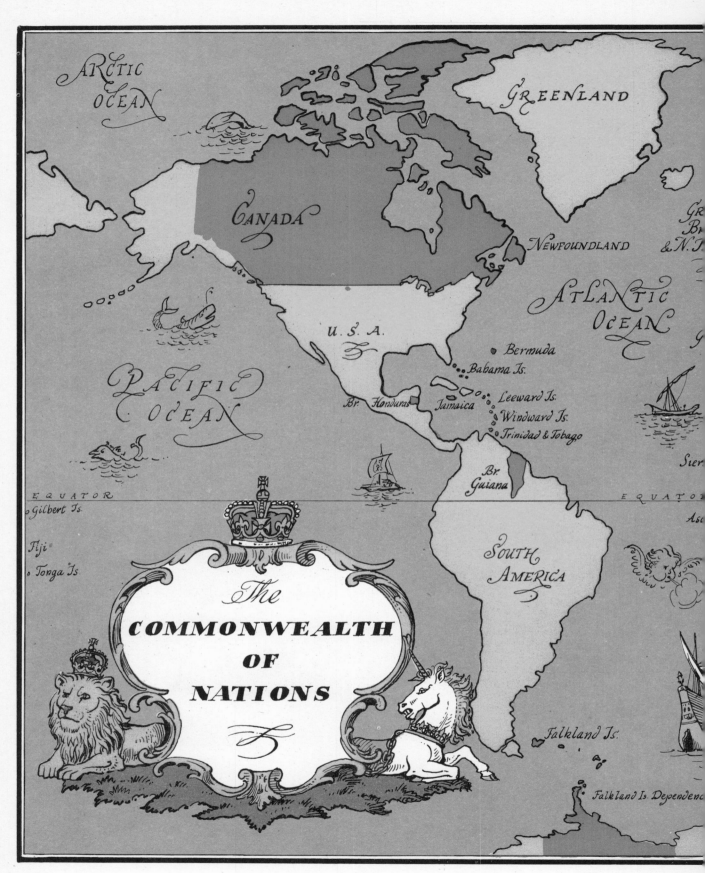

ARCTIC OCEAN

GREENLAND

CANADA

Newfoundland

GR.
Br.
& N.I.

ATLANTIC OCEAN

U.S.A.

Bermuda
Bahama Is.
Br. Honduras
Jamaica
Leeward Is.
Windward Is.
Trinidad & Tobago

PACIFIC OCEAN

Sier.

EQUATOR

Gilbert Is.

Fiji

Tonga Is.

Br. Guiana

EQUATOR

Asc.

SOUTH AMERICA

The
COMMONWEALTH
OF
NATIONS

Falkland Is.

Falkland Is. Dependenc

U. S. S. R.

ASIA

CHINA

EUROPE

AFRICA

Malta

Cyprus

Aden

PAKISTAN

INDIA

Hong Kong

Nigeria

GHANA

Cameroons

Somaliland
Protectorate

Ceylon

Fed. of
Malaya

BRUNEI

Sarawak

N. Borneo

New Guinea

Solomon
Is.

Ellice
Is.

Uganda

Kenya

Zanzibar

Seychelles

St. Helena

Tanganyika

Chagos Is

Christmas I.

New Hebrides

N. Rhodesia

Nyasaland

Mauritius

INDIAN
OCEAN

AUSTRALIA

Bechuanaland

Swaziland

Union of
South Africa

Basutoland

NEW
ZEALAND

TASMANIA

ANTARCTIC
OCEAN

NTARCTICA

One morning in January 1885, General Gordon, who had been defending Khartoum for 317 days, put on his uniform and sword, walked to the top of the Palace staircase, and as he looked down at the fierce mob of Dervishes beneath him was pierced by a spear and fell. The news of his death echoed round the world, for his fame extended far beyond Britain. He had conducted brilliant campaigns for the Emperor of China; the King of the Belgians and the Viceroy of India had asked for his help; and Egypt had made him Governor-General of the Sudan, which was then under her rule. There Gordon had fought the slave-trade. He once rode a camel 85 miles in 26 hours, entered a slave camp alone, and subdued the slave-traders with one glance of his strange, piercing blue eyes; it was said he wielded an almost magnetic power over men. When the Sudan was taken over by followers of the Mahdi, the Sudanese religious leader, Egypt called on Gordon to go to the rescue of her citizens. Gordon carried out his mission, but was cut off from help, and met his death. In the words of his friend Lord Cromer, 'he did not know what the word fear meant . . . he left a name that will be revered as long as the qualities of steadfast faith and indomitable courage have any hold on the feelings of mankind.'

A few years later British and Egyptian forces reconquered the Sudan and placed it under their joint Government. Many men from Britain went out to devote their lives to building the Sudan into a strong peaceful country; and so the Sudan, for part of its history, marched alongside the Commonwealth.

A Queen Elizabeth was on the throne when the British Empire put out its first roots, and another Queen—Victoria—reigned for a great part of the nineteenth century, when the Empire reached its greatest extent and began to turn into the Commonwealth of independent countries. Queen Victoria and Queen Elizabeth I were quite different in appearance, and whereas Elizabeth never married, Victoria had a husband to whom she was devoted, nine children and nineteen grandchildren. But if they were separated in time by three centuries, they were alike in having strong, determined characters, in commanding great affection from their subjects, and in achieving long and glorious reigns.

Queen Victoria first came to the throne at the age of eighteen. She was awakened from her sleep by two messengers who had galloped through the night to tell her she was Queen. She said simply, 'I will be good'; and from then on she devoted herself to the difficult task of reigning over a rapidly growing Empire. Like Elizabeth before her, Victoria took a great interest in all affairs of State, although, of course, she had far less real power. She had strong likes and dislikes, and if a Minister took a decision which displeased her, she would write him a long, vigorous and heavily underlined letter of protest.

It was during the reign of Queen Victoria that the Commonwealth and Empire increased its peoples from about 91 million to about 124 million; it was during her reign that the dominion of Canada was created, that New Zealand became part of the Commonwealth, and that the Australian Colonies united, and one of the proudest moments in Queen Victoria's life was when she assumed the title of Empress of India; she admired India and its people greatly, and even tried to learn Hindustani when she was an old lady. To many people in distant parts of the Empire, Victoria was an awesome and almost legendary figure. But though reigning over one of the greatest empires in the history of the world, she remained a person of simple tastes, who preferred living in an uncomfortable castle in Scotland, surrounded by her children and grandchildren, to the pomp and ceremony of the London court.

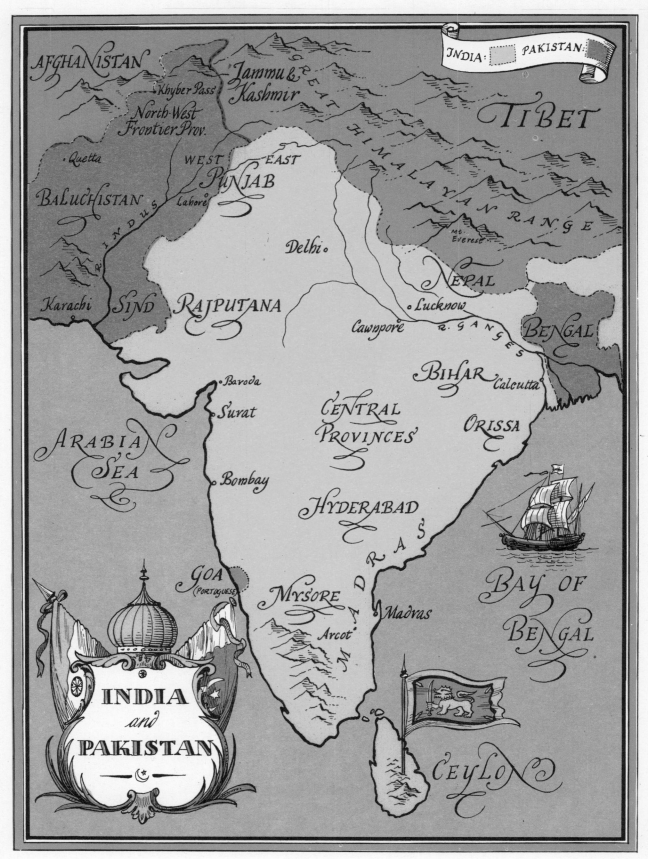

INDIA WAS the goal of those early explorers who accidentally stumbled across the New World in their search; it was India Christopher Columbus was hoping to find when he landed in the West Indies, and which the Portuguese sailors were seeking when they rounded the Cape of Good Hope for the first time; for India, with her bazaars full of gorgeous silks and calicoes, of jewels and spices, was a source of rich trade, as well as a strange and fascinating country. The first Englishmen to visit India were merchant adventurers, who made the long journey, partly by sea, partly by land, in the reign of Queen Elizabeth I. At that time India was ruled by the Moghuls, who had invaded the country from the north and were Moslems by religion. Their ruler, the Moghul Emperor, had a magnificent court. He had seven thrones, one wholly covered with diamonds, the others with rubies, emeralds and pearls. When Queen Elizabeth was told of the splendour of India, she granted a Royal Charter for the East India Company to be formed. At first, however, the Emperor would not let the English trade, so Sir Thomas Roe visited him to persuade him to change his mind. He took with him as presents a coach, a virginal (an Elizabethan musical instrument), a sword and a clock. With all of which the Emperor was delighted, and after some delays the required permission was granted.

The British built a trading factory at Surat, and soon the clerks were busily at work, sitting at their high, uncomfortable desks. And as in other parts of the Empire, small trading settlements grew quickly, and almost without anyone realising it, became towns and cities. In 1660, England was given Bombay as part of a dowry, and the merchants set to work to drain the swamps on which it stood and build a city. On the other side of India, Madras was bought from an Indian ruler; and a few years later Calcutta was founded on a desolate spot, till then inhabited by tigers and jackals and crocodiles, on the river Ganges. The French also established settlements in southern India, and it was not long before rivalry developed. The East India Company had never intended to do anything but trade by peaceful means; but in the eighteenth century, when France and England were fighting for supremacy in North America, the settlements in India were inevitably drawn into the struggle, and by taking opposite sides in the quarrels of Indian princes, began to fight each other.

In 1744 a young man called Robert Clive arrived in India to work for the East India Company as a clerk. He was bored with his work of writing out trading bills, but soon the struggle between France and England gave him his chance to prove himself, in William Pitt's words, a 'heaven-born general'. The French under their clever leader Dupleix had established an empire the size of France in southern India, and it looked as if they would drive the English out altogether, but their fortunes were turned against them by Clive's brilliant military skill. In a swift, daring attack, the young Captain frightened the enemy into abandoning the important town of Arcott, and then successfully held it for fifty-three

ROBERT, LORD CLIVE

days against an attacking force of 10,000 troops—despite the fact that the walls were in ruins and the garrison only consisted of 120 Europeans and 200 sepoys. Dupleix was recalled to France, and although the French sent out a formidable army during the Seven Years War, they were not a match for Clive, and gradually withdrew from India.

Meanwhile in Bengal, northern India, English influence was also growing; and in 1756 the Nawab of Bengal, anxious at the growth of English power, suddenly attacked and captured Calcutta. All the English men, women and children of the garrison were shut up in a tiny cell which became known as the 'Black Hole of Calcutta', for they were

imprisoned at the most sultry period of the year, and the following morning only 23 of the 146 who went in came out alive. Clive, however, recaptured Calcutta, routing an army of 34,000 with his small force of 600 British soldiers and 800 sepoys, while the following year he finally overwhelmed the Nawab's forces of 68,000 men at the battle of Plassey, with the loss of 'hardly a white soldier and twenty-two sepoys'. He rose to ever greater heights of wealth and power, and in 1765 he accepted from the Moghul Emperor the

46

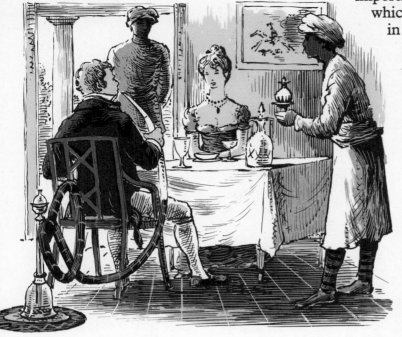

important position of *Diwan* of Bengal, which was an important development in the British administration of India.

Some of the merchants who went to India to work for the East India Company in the eighteenth century made huge fortunes, for in those days it was quite usual to accept bribes. Many of the Nabobs—as they were called—led lives of great luxury, were always in debt, and their amusements were mainly gossiping, playing cards, driving in their grand carriages, and perhaps watching an elephant fight. The gentlemen liked to smoke a hookah, inhaling a mixture of tobacco, herbs, sugar and spice through the long pipe, which was arranged by a special hookah servant. And woe betide anyone who stepped over another man's hookah pipe, for that was an insult, and meant a duel. At home in England, however, the Nabob's great wealth was disapproved of, and the British Government realised that the Company had gained far too much power for a private concern; so a law was passed which brought it under some control by Parliament.

Clive, before he retired, began to take steps to prevent corruption in the Company's employees, and Warren Hastings, who succeeded him as Governor-General of Bengal, continued this work. Hastings was undoubtedly one of the greatest of India's governors. No Englishman has probably ever understood the Indian character so well, and he took a great interest in India's literature and art—he is known to have translated Indian epic poems into English verse while travelling on his duties around Bengal. His two greatest achievements were the plans he made for the government of the country and his brilliant conduct of the war against the Mahrattas when he saved the British from being driven out of India. However, he made many and powerful enemies and on his return to England he was brought to trial on charges of corruption. The trial became famous, for it dragged on for seven long years, before Hastings was finally acquitted; and not until many years after did the ungrateful government acknowledge his great service to his own country and to India.

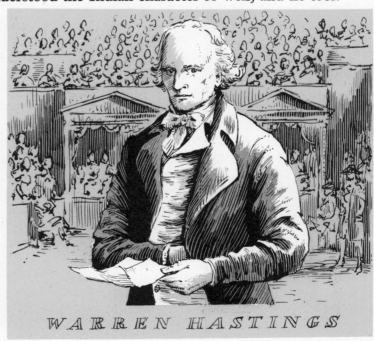

WARREN HASTINGS

47

The men who followed Clive and Hastings in working for the East India Company continued to extend its domains until they included all India except certain States under their own Maharajahs or Princes; and the Company grew into a great government and Civil Service, which ruled India until Queen Victoria was on the throne. It carried out many reforms, introduced the railway and telegram, made canals, founded schools and instituted a 'penny post'. But the Company's rule had defects as well as good points, and some of the changes they made offended Indians. In 1857 a Mutiny of sepoy troops broke out, in which there was much bloodshed on both sides. The Mutiny convinced Britain that the Company's rule should come to an end, and India was placed under the protection of the Crown. Queen Victoria issued a proclamation, on the occasion, in which she granted amnesty to those who had taken part in the Mutiny; for she was anxious to heal the wounds of the recent strife. In 1877 she assumed the title 'Empress of India', and this special link with the Crown continued for many years. When King Edward VII succeeded Victoria to the throne he visited India to attend a magnificent Durbar for his Coronation; and so, some years later, did King George V. He was the last King-Emperor to do so, for when India became independent, she and Pakistan chose to become Republics, while recognising the Queen as the head of the Commonwealth. India's movement towards independence was led by her great religious leader, Mahatma Gandhi; both Britain and India were anxious that India should become independent, especially after the Second World War, but one great difficulty lay in the differences between the two main religions, Islam and Hinduism. This problem was eventually solved by creating two different States from what had been British India—Pakistan, mainly Moslem; and India, mainly Hindu; and in 1947 these two countries joined the Commonwealth as fully independent members.

48

Many legends are told about Ceylon. One says that Ceylon was first inhabited by dragons, with whom the merchants of the neighbouring countries came to trade; and when they saw how beautiful it was, they stayed and peopled the island. Ancient legend also surrounds Ceylon's great mountain, Adam's Peak, regarded as holy by Moslems, Hindus and Christians. The Buddhists believe that Buddha himself left his footprints on Adam's Peak; early travellers from Europe, however, thought that the mountain contained the remains of Adam, who landed in Ceylon when he was cast out of Paradise. Some say Adam's tears turned into a great lake; others that they miraculously became precious stones, for Ceylon has always been famous for her jewels, which were bought even by the Emperors of China. These legends show how many threads are woven into Ceylon's history, for she has been invaded by many different races: first came Aryans from India, whose descendants are the Sinhalese today; from India, too, came Tamils who now form a section of Ceylon's inhabitants.

In the sixteenth century the Portuguese invaded Ceylon; to be followed one hundred and fifty years later by the Dutch. Finally when Holland and Britain were at war at the end of the eighteenth century, Britain captured the island. Britain was only at first concerned with the coastal part of Ceylon, and the Kingdom of Kandy, in the heart of Ceylon, remained independent. The Kandyans eventually made a treaty with Britain, and the whole of Ceylon became a British colony. An important event in founding Ceylon's prosperity took place towards the end of the nineteenth century. Until then Ceylon had been growing important crops of coffee, but a serious disease suddenly attacked and ruined all the coffee plants. The head of the Royal Botanic Gardens at Kandy therefore persuaded the planters to lay out fields of tea plants instead. The new tea industry grew with amazing speed, and today tea is still Ceylon's most important crop. Ceylon remained a colony until 1947 when she followed close in the steps of India and Pakistan, to become an independent member of the Commonwealth.

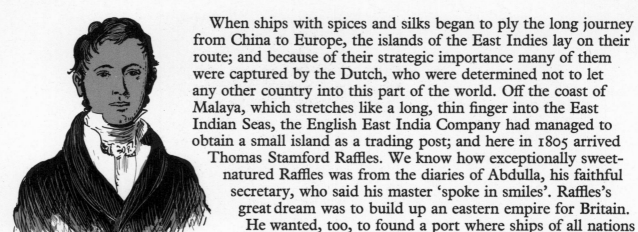

Thomas Stamford Raffles

When ships with spices and silks began to ply the long journey from China to Europe, the islands of the East Indies lay on their route; and because of their strategic importance many of them were captured by the Dutch, who were determined not to let any other country into this part of the world. Off the coast of Malaya, which stretches like a long, thin finger into the East Indian Seas, the English East India Company had managed to obtain a small island as a trading post; and here in 1805 arrived Thomas Stamford Raffles. We know how exceptionally sweet-natured Raffles was from the diaries of Abdulla, his faithful secretary, who said his master 'spoke in smiles'. Raffles's great dream was to build up an eastern empire for Britain. He wanted, too, to found a port where ships of all nations might come and trade. But where? The Dutch held all the best harbours. Then he had a brilliant idea. At the tip of Malaya lay a swampy, forgotten, almost uninhabited island, Singapore. Raffles visited it and negotiated with its ruler for its cession, and almost overnight, thanks to his efforts, a flourishing city and port grew up. Today Singapore, which is a British colony with its own government, is one of the most important ports in the world.

Raffles was tireless in his work for Singapore and Malaya; but many misfortunes befell him. His health was ruined; his wife and three children died; and on his return to England his ship caught fire, and all the writings, drawings and botanical and zoological specimens he had patiently collected were destroyed. Before he died, not long after his return to England, he founded the London Zoo.

On the mainland of Malaya four British settlements developed which were called, with Singapore, the Straits Settlements. The rest of Malaya was ruled by Malay Sultans, with whom Britain had treaties of protection and friendship. In 1948 the Malay settlements and States joined together in the Federation of Malaya, and in 1957 the Federation became an independent member of the Commonwealth.

To the east of Malaya and south of the South
China Sea lie the many islands of the East Indies,
once part of a lost continent that sank into the sea until only the top of its mountains
were left. One of these islands is Borneo, on which are three British colonies, Brunei,
North Borneo and Sarawak. Until the beginning of the nineteenth century very little
was known about Borneo, but one day a young man called James Brooke arrived
determined to find out more about the mysterious country. Brooke found Borneo
in a state of war, for the Dyak tribes were in rebellion against their Malay overlords.
He made friends with Hassim, the ruler of Sarawak, and helped him to quell the
rebellion, for which Hassim was so grateful that he made Brooke Rajah of Sarawak.
The 'White Rajah' set to work to govern Sarawak firmly but kindly. First of all he
attacked and defeated the pirates who were the terror of the rest of Sarawak. When they
swept down on their victims in their long, low *prahus*, brandishing their sharp, crescent-
shaped *krisses*, no man, woman or child was safe, and they were never caught for they
quickly disappeared among the creeks and inlets of many-rivered Borneo. With the help
of Captain Keppel, who later became a famous admiral, Brooke managed to break up
their strongholds.

Brooke's many adventures were still by no means yet over, however. His old friend
Hassim was attacked by enemies in Brunei one night, and rather than surrender to them,
he destroyed himself and his family by blowing up his house, after sending a message
and a ring to Brooke. When Brooke heard of Hassim's death he sailed at once to Brunei
and attacked the town. The guilty Sultan fled, and as a result of his defeat ceded to
Brooke the island of Labuan, which, like Sarawak, has remained British since. Rajah
Brooke continued to govern Sarawak, until, as an old man, he returned to England.
When he died his title passed on to his nephew, Sir Charles Brooke, who continued his
uncle's good government for fifty years. And by the time the third white Rajah succeeded
his father in 1917, even the Dyak's cherished custom of head hunting had almost stopped.
After the Second World War the Rajah decided that the British Crown would be better
able to assume Sarawak protection and progress than his own family, and he therefore
handed over his country to Britain to become a Crown Colony in 1946; in the same year,
too, North Borneo, which until then had been administered by a private company, also
became a British colony.

51

AUSTRALIA was the last continent in the world to be discovered, a strange fact, considering that from ancient times learned geographers had argued very convincingly that somewhere in the great, magic south seas some such continent was to be found; but since nobody had ever seen it they just wrote boldly across the bottom of their maps 'Terra Australis Incognita'—'Unknown South Land'. Fantastic notions were spun about it, some people actually believing that its inhabitants walked about on their heads. From the seventeenth century onwards, however, ships sailing on a southerly course would occasionally sight or land on parts of the South Land, and very slowly and gradually Australia's outline was pieced together. The Dutch made discoveries on the west coast, which they called New Holland; and in 1642 Tasman discovered the island of Tasmania, and landed for the first time in New Zealand.

The first Englishman to sail to the South Land was a bold, adventurous buccaneer, William Dampier, who had spent his life until then plundering unwary ships for treasure. Adventures and strange occurrences followed Dampier wherever he went; he claimed that in Australia he and his men once opened a shark to eat it and found a whole hippopotamus inside; while he has left us one of the first descriptions of a kangaroo. Yet the tales which travellers from the South Land brought back of strange animals, fierce aborigines and dangerous coral reefs do not seem to have unduly impressed the stay-at-homes, until, about seventy years after Dampier's adventures, Captain Cook appears on the scene.

Luck did not make Captain Cook; he became a great explorer entirely by his own genius and hard work, for he was the son of a farm labourer, and started life as a stable boy. But he longed to go to sea, and his great chance came when England was fighting France in the Seven Years War. Cook volunteered for service in the Royal Navy and helped in the attack and capture of Quebec. Soon he was given the task of surveying the coast of Newfoundland, which he did so well that in 1768 the honour came to him of commanding an expedition to Tahiti to record the transit of Venus across the sun. Commanding the *Endeavour*, Cook reached Tahiti and carried out his commission. Next, he sailed southwards, and landed on the east coast of North Island, New Zealand. Cook sailed on south, charting the coast with his patient accuracy—many of his charts are still in use today—until, as Cape Turnagain tells us by its name, he turned round and sailed north again. He finally sailed round both North and South Island. Then, leaving New

Zealand at Cape Farewell, Cook sailed due west, and nineteen days later, early one April morning in 1770, land appeared. Delighted, Cook and his companions, the first men to land on Australia's east coast, explored Botany Bay, given its name because Sir Joseph Banks, their naturalist, found so many plants there to add to his collection. Then they sailed on up the coast, but nearly lost their precious ship when it hit what sailors now know to avoid—the Barrier Reef. Fortunately the *Endeavour* floated off and eventually reached home safely.

Besides his discoveries Cook was also the first man to fight successfully the dreadful disease of scurvy, which up till then had killed many sailors. He was a brilliant commander, well-loved by the men who served under him, while he was also always very gentle with the people of the lands he visited, so it is doubly sad that on the island of Hawaii, he and a party of marines were attacked by natives of the island, and the 'celebrated circumnavigator' was clubbed to death and 'fell into the water and spoke no more'.

Several years after Cook's death his friend Joseph Banks suggested to the British Government that it should put the land Cook had discovered to some useful purpose. The Government's idea of a useful purpose was to found a penal settlement there, and in 1787 a fleet of eleven ships with one thousand people left England. Many were convicts, but not necessarily criminals, because the laws of punishment were very much more severe than they are now. The men and women who crowded the decks as they approached this unknown new country were luckier than they knew in having as their first Governor-General, Captain Arthur Phillip. Phillip, following Cook's writings, headed for Botany Bay, but came to the conclusion that it was too swampy and exposed a place to found his colony. So he surveyed the coast in an open boat, until, in his words, he 'had the satisfaction of finding the finest harbour in the world in which a thousand of the line may ride in perfect security'.

Here, 'near the run of fresh water, which stole silently along through a very thick wood', the Union Jack was hoisted as the guns gave a salute; and here today stands the magnificent city of Sydney.

PHILLIP

Having landed, Phillip was faced with a gigantic task; he had to keep law and order among difficult men, to encourage them to build, dig and plant, so that they could have a roof over their heads and food to eat. He had to contend with an unknown climate which destroyed the crops, and with sickness and famine among the settlers. To all these tasks he proved more than equal. From the beginning he had decided that Australia was to be a free, democratic nation, and under his just and benevolent law even those that were still serving sentences were happy. Having founded New South Wales, he sailed back to England worn out by his work, and died in 1792. Few of his fellow-countrymen at that time can have guessed though, that Australia was to become possibly 'the most valuable acquisition Great Britain ever made'.

When, seven years after the foundation of Sydney, Governor Phillip retired, a new governor replaced him from England, and on his ship were a midshipman, Matthew Flinders, and a surgeon, George Bass. Eager to explore their new country, they took a little boat only eight feet long, the *Tom Thumb*, and surveyed much of the coast of New South Wales. Bass also sailed through the strait which bears his name, so proving that Tasmania was an island, and he was the first to sight the coast of what was to become the state of Victoria; not many years after this the fine harbour on which Melbourne was to grow up was discovered. And in 1803, in a boat considered quite unseaworthy, Flinders sailed right round Australia, proving at last beyond doubt that it was an island-continent. It was Flinders, too, who first thought of a name to replace the rather long *Terra Australis*, suggesting that it be converted into Australia, 'as being more agreeable to the ear'. A few years later the great Governor Macquarie, who turned Sydney from a weak settlement into a flourishing colony by building roads, bridges, a church and several townships, asked that in future the name Australia should be used in all official despatches, and the name had come to stay.

Meanwhile, the Australians, although they were learning something about their coasts, were still hemmed into the west by the steep and thickly forested Blue Mountains. They were especially anxious to find more land, since, thanks to John Macarthur, who had cross-bred several types of sheep and produced a hardy breed, Australia's first flocks of sheep were multiplying rapidly and needed new ground for grazing. So, again in Governor Macquarie's time, the settlers crossed the Blue Mountains for the first time, and saw on the other side mile upon mile of rich pasture land. After this, many explorers, some famous, and others quite unknown, set out to discover their country, sometimes worn out by heat and hunger, sometimes attacked by hostile bands of aborigines, but always drawn on to know what lay beyond the horizon.

FLINDERS

55

Through the nineteenth century and into the twentieth the work of exploring and building the Australian nation went on. Besides New South Wales, Victoria and the island of Tasmania, four other states or territories came into being. Western Australia was founded on Christmas Day 1826, when a small company of soldiers took possession of St. George's Sound on its coast. Captain James Stirling became its first Governor-General and chose the site of the port of Fremantle and the capital city of Perth. The great explorer Stuart, who rowed hundreds of back-breaking miles on the Darling and Murray rivers, led exploration to South Australia, and when he heard of the discovery of the site of Adelaide, he suggested that it was a spot where the colonist 'might venture with every prospect of success', so 546 settlers arrived there in 1836. And now explorers began to penetrate into the vast Northern Territory. In 1860 John Stuart planted the Union Jack in the heart of Australia, and a year later the whole continent was first crossed from south to north. Finally, Queensland, the youngest of Australia's states, was created in 1859.

Australia's population continued to increase and her sheep farms to multiply. Then came a discovery which caused another flow of immigrants. Gold was found in New South Wales, Victoria and Queensland, and far away in the middle of the parched deserts of Western Australia. Here sunburnt 'diggers', sheath-knives and revolvers stuck into the sashes at their waists, broad felt hats on their heads, pushed their way into lonely country. Some nearly died of thirst; some, too, made huge fortunes; one 'digger' who had struck rich had his horse shod in gold. All the states progressed with amazing speed, and towards the end of the nineteenth century they realised that the time was ripe for them to join together into one united country; a federal constitution was agreed on, and on 1st January 1901 the Commonweath of Australia came into being.

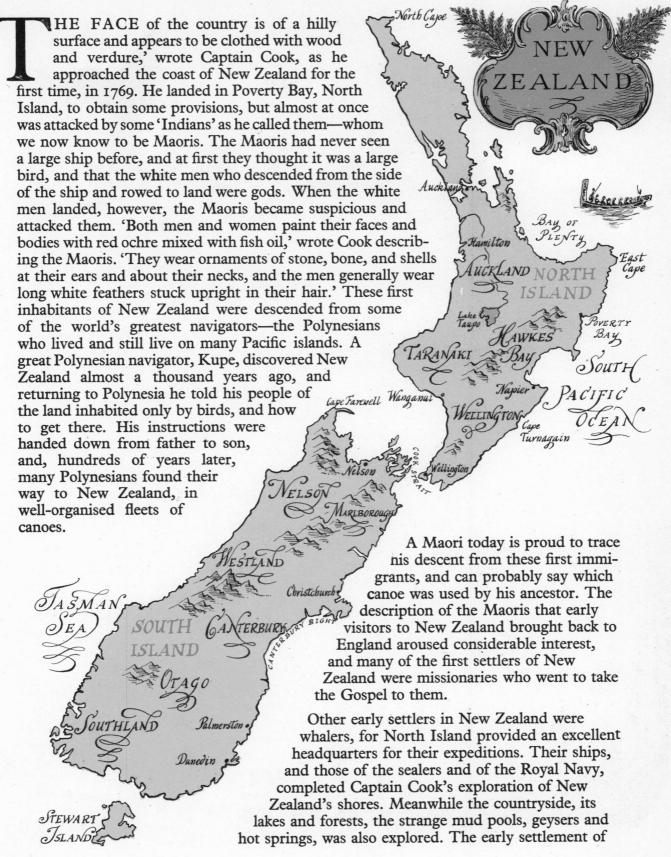

'THE FACE of the country is of a hilly surface and appears to be clothed with wood and verdure,' wrote Captain Cook, as he approached the coast of New Zealand for the first time, in 1769. He landed in Poverty Bay, North Island, to obtain some provisions, but almost at once was attacked by some 'Indians' as he called them—whom we now know to be Maoris. The Maoris had never seen a large ship before, and at first they thought it was a large bird, and that the white men who descended from the side of the ship and rowed to land were gods. When the white men landed, however, the Maoris became suspicious and attacked them. 'Both men and women paint their faces and bodies with red ochre mixed with fish oil,' wrote Cook describing the Maoris. 'They wear ornaments of stone, bone, and shells at their ears and about their necks, and the men generally wear long white feathers stuck upright in their hair.' These first inhabitants of New Zealand were descended from some of the world's greatest navigators—the Polynesians who lived and still live on many Pacific islands. A great Polynesian navigator, Kupe, discovered New Zealand almost a thousand years ago, and returning to Polynesia he told his people of the land inhabited only by birds, and how to get there. His instructions were handed down from father to son, and, hundreds of years later, many Polynesians found their way to New Zealand, in well-organised fleets of canoes.

A Maori today is proud to trace his descent from these first immigrants, and can probably say which canoe was used by his ancestor. The description of the Maoris that early visitors to New Zealand brought back to England aroused considerable interest, and many of the first settlers of New Zealand were missionaries who went to take the Gospel to them.

Other early settlers in New Zealand were whalers, for North Island provided an excellent headquarters for their expeditions. Their ships, and those of the sealers and of the Royal Navy, completed Captain Cook's exploration of New Zealand's shores. Meanwhile the countryside, its lakes and forests, the strange mud pools, geysers and hot springs, was also explored. The early settlement of

57

New Zealand was quite haphazard; not until 1840 did the British Government, encouraged by a great believer in planned colonisation, Gibbon Wakefield, take over responsibility for New Zealand and plan to send it immigrants. But now the Maoris grew very alarmed at the rapid increase of the white man. In North Island, they set up a king, and a struggle with the settlers broke out which lasted for nearly ten years. The Maoris were chivalrous fighters, who often send food and ammunition to their enemies if they were weakened, so that the combat should be equal. When peace was made the settlers, in their turn, showed great concern for the Maoris' welfare, and today Maoris and British-descended New Zealanders live amicably together.

Although gold was found at Otago in 1861 and at Westland three years later, which led thousands of Australian miners to come to the country; owing to the almost ideal climate, farming—in particular sheep farming—has always been the principal industry of New Zealand; the prosperity of the country largely depending on her exports of mutton, wool, and dairy produce.

Like Australia, New Zealand was managing her own affairs from such an early stage in her history that for a long time it did not occur to the British Government to legalise the position; but in 1931 the Statute of Westminster stated that Australia, New Zealand, and other Dominions were, by law, what they had long been in fact, independent members of the Commonwealth.

Of all the many ways in which countries have come into the Commonwealth, none can be odder than the story of the far-distant island of Pitcairn. In 1787 His Majesty's ship the *Bounty*, under the command of Captain Bligh, set sail for Tahiti, to collect a cargo of bread-fruit plants. Opinions differ about Captain Bligh's character. Some think he was exceptionally harsh, and cruel, and others that he kept no stricter discipline than was usual in the Royal Navy at that time. Whatever the case, when his ship at last reached Tahiti, his men were already discontented, and when, after twenty-three delightful weeks on Tahiti, they set sail again, some of the officers and men, led by the master's mate, Fletcher Christian, rose in mutiny. Bligh, awakened from his sleep to find, to his amazement, men all about him armed with cutlasses and pistols, was forced to board the launch with eighteen other men, and the mutineers flung after them a few pieces of pork and some other provisions. They little thought their hated captain would survive, but Bligh's great skill as a navigator did not desert him even in these circumstances; he forced an iron discipline on to his eighteen men, and through storms, shark-infested seas and every kind of danger and hardship sailed 3,600 miles, one of the longest journeys ever made in an open boat.

Bligh eventually returned to Tahiti in pursuit of the mutineers; but they were nowhere to be found. For, stopping there only to take on board some Tahitian girls as their wives, they had sailed away again until they came to the small, remote, rocky island of Pitcairn. There they had landed, set fire to the *Bounty*, and remained hidden from the world; until one day eighteen years later a chance ship sighted them, and solved the mystery that had been puzzling everyone in Britain for so long. Today Pitcairn is still inhabited by some of the descendants of those bygone mutineers of the *Bounty*.

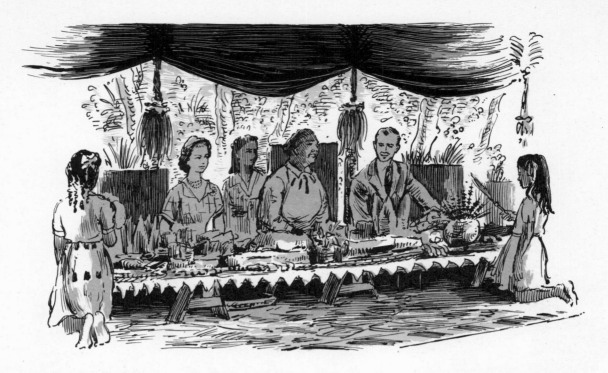

The Pacific Ocean has several thousand islands over its vast expanse, islands with cloudless skies, brilliant flowers, and palm-fringed lagoons. They are divided into three main groups—'Black Islands' (Melanesia), 'Small Islands' (Micronesia), and 'Many Islands' (Polynesia), and many from each group are dependencies of Britain, Australia or New Zealand. The largest group is the Colony of Fiji, the main islands of which were actually discovered by the desperate Captain Bligh and his eighteen men. Bligh roughly charted thirty-nine of the Fijian Islands, and for a time they were called 'Bligh's Islands'. Later they asked to be taken into the British Empire, and the King of Fiji sent his war club to Queen Victoria, capped with a silver crown. Then there are the Gilbert and Ellice Islands, the New Hebrides—the only island to be both French and British at the same time, for it is ruled by both countries under a special agreement—and the British Solomon Islands, which were originally discovered by a Spaniard.

Finally there is the kingdom of Tonga, which is independent, but protected by Britain under a special treaty. Queen Salote of Tonga has been specially loved in Britain since she went to London to attend the Coronation of Queen Elizabeth. As the Coronation passed through the streets of London it was raining, but Queen Salote refused to put up the cover over her carriage, and waved to the crowds as the rain poured over her, a magnificent gesture that they have never forgotten. Not long after, Queen Elizabeth paid a return visit to Tonga on her Commonwealth Tour. She was shown the dignified tortoise, Tu'i Malila, which was presented to a Tongan Chief by Captain Cook in 1777, and still lives in Queen Salote's palace grounds. Queen Elizabeth was also entertained to a grand banquet, where the guests, in the tradition of Tonga, sat cross-legged on the ground, garlanded with flowers, and feasted on roast sucking-pig, crayfish, lobsters, chickens and yams.

In the Indian Ocean are also islands within the Commonwealth: Mauritius and the Seychelles, both captured by Britain from France during the war against Napoleon. In the Indian Ocean, too, is the British Colony and Protectorate of Aden, the hot, dry peninsula on the coast of Arabia.

There are many other islands and outposts in the Commonwealth. In the Mediterranean there are the rock fortress of Gibraltar, captured by Britain from Spain in 1704, and the islands of Malta and Cyprus. Malta holds the George Cross, which she was awarded for the great courage with which she resisted heavy bombardment in the Second World War. The beautiful island of Cyprus was once captured by Richard Cœur de Lion, and then became part of the Turkish Empire until Turkey ceded it to Britain in 1878. Far away on the other side of the world is Hong Kong, which China gave to Britain by treaty in 1842. In the South Atlantic Ocean are the remote islands of Ascension, Tristan de Cunha and St. Helena—where Napoleon spent the last years of his life. And right at the tip of South America lie the Falkland Islands. They are the southernmost inhabited British possessions, but there are vast dependencies even farther south in Antarctica.

Here Captain Scott struggled against ice and blizzards to reach the South Pole; on the return journey he and his men died one by one, Oates even choosing to go out and meet death rather than be a burden on his companions. 'Had we but lived,' wrote Scott in his diary, 'I should have had a tale to tell of the hardihood, endurance and courage of my companions which would have stirred the heart of every Englishman. These rough notes and our dead bodies must tell the tale. . . .' Scott's spirit of adventure and courage has not died in the Commonwealth. In 1957 a joint Commonwealth Antartic Expedition set out; and on 19th January 1958 Sir Edmund Hillary of New Zealand, the conqueror of Mount Everest, and Dr. Vivian Fuchs of Britain, having successfully completed their journeys, met and shook hands at the South Pole.

CANADA

AUSTRALIA

NEW ZEALAND

INDIA

That is the story of the Commonwealth—or rather part of the story, for it has many more tales of pioneers, explorers and builders, many more hard-won battles, discoveries and strange coincidences than could fit into a book ten times this size. The story of the Commonwealth during the two great world wars 1914–18 and 1939–45, for example, has not been mentioned, nor the heroism of Commonwealth soldiers from every part of the world. Both the wars started in Europe, far away from many of the Commonwealth countries, yet when Hitler invaded Poland in 1939 he must have been surprised to learn that, thousands of miles across the world, such countries as Australia and Canada should have decided that it was just as much their concern to join Britain in the fight against dictatorship, as if they had been in immediate danger of invasion. The reasons for their action are not so surprising when the whole history of the countries of the Commonwealth is taken into account. Because they have so long been associated together by their own free will, Commonwealth countries have developed the same beliefs in just,

SOUTH AFRICA

CENTRAL AFRICA

EAST AFRICA

CARIBBEAN

PAKISTAN
CEYLON
GHANA
MALAYA

democratic government, and are ready to defend their beliefs with their lives if necessary. That is why, though they disagree as much as they like in less important matters, they always rally together in times of danger.

But it is not by any means only in war that the people of the Commonwealth work closely together. They help each other in many different ways, in scientific work, in education, in lending money for important developments; and, of course, they meet in sport. Once every four years the British Empire and Commonwealth Games are held in one of the capitals of the Commonwealth, and in between, many other contests are held, especially in Rugby football, and cricket, two games played almost exclusively within the Commonwealth.

In 1953 the Head of the Commonwealth, Queen Elizabeth II, started the longest Commonwealth Royal Tour so far undertaken. Like Drake so many hundreds of years ago, in the reign of the first Queen Elizabeth, Her Majesty circumnavigated the globe,

CYPRUS
NORTH BORNEO
SARAWAK
PACIFIC ISLANDS

but of course her ships and planes carried her very much faster than the gallant *Golden Hind* could travel. First the Queen went to the island founded by a shipwreck, Bermuda; then on to Jamaica, the gay calypso-island; across the Pacific, the Queen's next stops were Fiji and Tonga. Then came her tour of New Zealand, during which she gave her annual Christmas Broadcast, usually transmitted from Britain. In February 1954 she went on to visit Australia, the first reigning monarch to do so. In Australia the Queen and Prince Philip spent two happy months, greeted everywhere they went by cheering crowds, and seeing some of the features of Australian life, from exhibitions by life-savers to the Flying Doctor's Service, from a 'Dance of the Wallaby' to a University Students' Rag. Homeward bound, the Queen visited the Cocos-Keeling Islands, the beautiful island of Ceylon, Aden and Uganda with its many chiefs and kingdoms. Lastly, as the Royal Yacht neared home, the Royal Party stopped at Gibraltar and Malta. When the Queen finally reached home again, she had been away six months and travelled 50,000 miles. Yet even then, of course, she had seen only a portion of the wonders of the Commonwealth, and met only a few of its millions of friendly people; but she had seen everywhere something far more important—the spirit of kinship and friendship which links the Commonwealth together, and which was first sown hundreds of years ago by adventurous men seeking new lands where freedom and happiness could flourish.

This book is printed in four colours by photolithography by Jarrold and Sons Limited at the Empire Press in Norwich

A
F
746.46 Fisher, Katharine

Quilting in squares

© THE BAKER & TAYLOR CO.

QUILTING
IN
SQUARES

Barker + Taylor
Nov 1984

QUILTING
IN
SQUARES

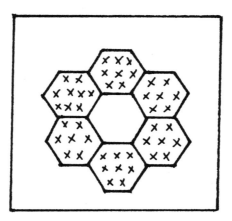

Katharine Fisher
and Elizabeth Kay

Illustrated with Diagrams

CHARLES SCRIBNER'S SONS
NEW YORK

8516

We would like to thank our friends and students who
were kind enough to lend us some of the squares and
quilts appearing in this book:
Lois Harman, B. L. Buck, Nancy Ryan,
Susan Luchetti, and Betty Dominick.

New Canaan Quilters:

Ann Akitt, Jan Moller, Ann Price, Ellen Warden,
Mary Wagner, Val Erichs, Carolyn Scott, Beth Bodnar,
Wendy Stone, Ann Hummel, Nancy Rodts, Carol
Kohler, Nancy Longley, Dorie Peck, Margaret Smith,
Janet Johnson, Concie Hershey, Kristin Johnston,
Barbara Kries, Joan Hutchinson, Mary Bartlett, Carole
Clarkson, Ann Thornton, Shannon Weideman,
and Nancy Thompson.

Pictures: *Robert Fearon*
           David Kay
           Jonathan Kay
Diagrams: *Katharine Fisher*
Color photography: *Russ Kinne*

Library of Congress Cataloging in Publication Data
Fisher, Katharine.
    Quilting in squares.

    1. Quilting.   I. Kay, Elizabeth, joint author.
II. Title.
TT835.F57   746.4'6   77-16137
ISBN 0-684-15501-X

1 3 5 7 9 11 13 15 17 19 MD/C 20 18 16 14 12 10 8 6 4 2
Printed in the United States of America

*To Walt and Kit for their patience and
encouragement; to Connie, Sarah, and
Lowrie for their enthusiasm from afar; and
to my mother.*

*To Andy, David, Jim, and Jonathan, who never
tired of taking pictures of quilts, and to Lynn,
who assured me it was all possible. What fun
we had!*

Contents

◤◥◤◥◤◥◤◥◤◥

QUILTING
IN
SQUARES

INTRODUCTION

Quilts are a part of our American heritage. Today's quilts will be tomorrow's heirlooms! Be a part of this and have fun in the process. The old quilt-making method involved large frames and many people to complete a quilt. This is not practical for our life-style today. We will show you how to make a quilt by yourself, following the easy diagrams and instructions. This method is quilting in squares; your quilt can be carried around with you like needlepoint or knitting. You can enjoy sewing when you are waiting in carpools, sitting in meetings, or relaxing at home.

We have three traditional quilts to tell you about. The first is patchwork, which is the easiest and shows you tricks you will use in the other two. Next is appliqué, which is fun and creative. Piecework is the third and is very challenging. Further fun will be learning biscuits, "Crazy Patch," and a really quick confidence-builder, the tied quilt.

FACTS AND FABRICS

Make life easy by buying the right fabrics; 100 percent cotton, calico, muslin, gingham, and Dacron and cotton blends are the best. They hold a fold and are not flimsy or slippery.

Yes—you *must* wash, dry, and press your fabrics before using them. Avoid the heartbreak of shrinkage, running colors, and too much sizing (that shiny surface on new material).

Batting is the filler inside the quilt. It comes in various sizes and thicknesses and can be purchased along with your fabric.

HERE ARE THE SQUARES—TAKE YOUR PICK AND BEGIN

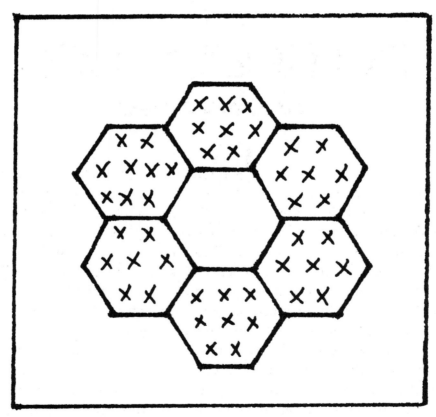

Figure 1   Patchwork

Figure 2

Patchwork

Figure 3

Appliqué

Figure 4

Appliqué

Figure 5

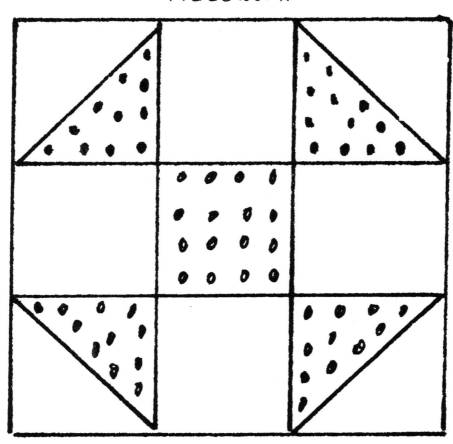

Piecework

Figure 6

YOU HAVE PICKED A PATTERN—WHAT ABOUT THE SIZE?

Here are *mattress* sizes:

Bassinet   36 inches wide by 36 inches long
Crib   40 inches wide by 60 inches long
Twin   39 inches wide by 72 inches long
Double   54 inches wide by 72 inches long
Queen   60 inches wide by 80 inches long

The size of a quilt is the mattress size plus the overhang (*Figure 7*).

All quilts have top squares and back squares. These may also be referred to as blocks. Top squares may be any size, but 9-inch to 14-inch squares are the easiest to work with.

Quilt edges are usually finished with strips or borders.

We will show you two different ways to make the back of your quilt. In the first you will have the same number of back squares as

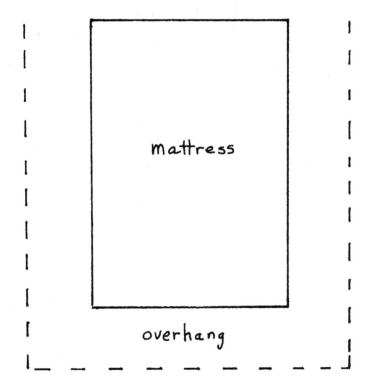

Figure 7

top squares, but the backs will be cut ½ inch larger to make it easier to join the seams later.

In the second method you will cut much larger back squares. These will be the size of four top squares joined together. The larger back square can be used only when there is an *even* number of squares (or blocks) in the quilt. See Plates 1 and 2.

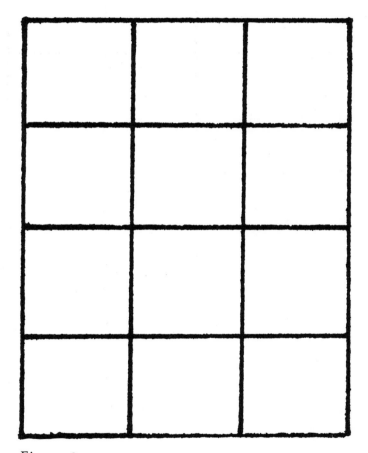

Figure 8

Figure 8 shows a quilt made up of *odd* numbers of top squares in the width and the same number of back squares.

Figure 9 shows a quilt made up of an *even* number of top squares using the larger back squares.

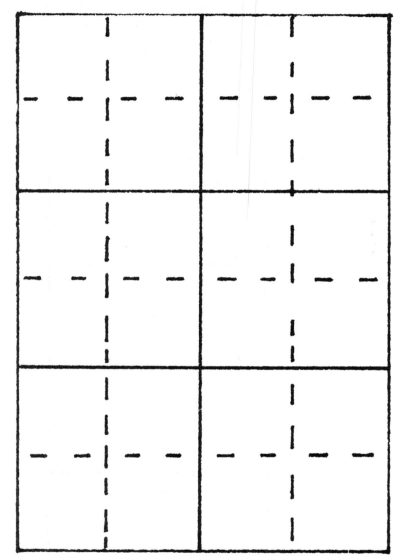

Figure 9

Quilts are not bedspreads. If you are planning a bedspread you must allow for a pillow tuck. This is done by making the quilt longer.

You have picked the type of quilt you are going to make. You have decided how you will make the back of the quilt. You must now decide whether you will finish the edges with strips or with borders. Strips are easy and are what we recommend for a first quilt. Borders are wider, need batting, and must be quilted. If you are planning borders you should use the cutting guide for borders shown on page 24.

IF ARITHMETIC TURNS YOU OFF—here are some charts to help you see how many squares you'll need for the quilt top and back, and the amount of fabric you will need to buy *(Figures 10, 11, 12)*.

Measurement Chart

	Over-hang	Square Size	Top Squares Needed	Back Squares Needed	If Using Large Back Squares	Final Quilt Measurement
Bassinet 36″ x 36″	None	9″ x 9″	4 across 4 down	4 across 4 down	2—18″ x 18″	36″ x 36″
Crib 40″ x 60″	None	10″ x 10″	4 across 6 down	4 across 6 down	6—20″ x 20″	40″ x 60″
Twin 39″ x 72″	13″	13″ x 13″	4 across 6 down	4 across 6 down	6—26″ x 26″	52″ x 78″
Double 54″ x 72″	9″	12″ x 12″	6 across 8 down	6 across 8 down	12—24″ x 24″	72″ x 96″
Queen 60″ x 80″	10″	13″ x 13″	6 across 8 down	6 across 8 down	12—26″ x 26″	78″ x 104″

Figure 10

Fabric for Patchwork or Appliqué Patterns

Roughly estimate the amount of fabric used in each square, keeping in mind the number of squares in the quilt. Don't forget to use your scrap bag!

Fabric Chart for Quilts
For Top and Back Only

	For the Top	*For the Back*
Bassinet	1¼ yards	1¼ yards
Crib	2 yards	2 yards
Twin	4 yards	4 yards
Double	5½ yards	5½ yards
Queen	6 yards	6 yards

Figure 11

Bedspreads—Squares and Fabric Needed

	Top	Back	If Using Large Back Squares	Fabric Needed	
				Top	Back
Twin	4 across 8 down	4 across 8 down	2 across 4 down	5½ yards	5½ yards
Double	6 across 8 down	6 across 8 down	3 across 4 down	6 yards	6 yards
Queen	6 across 10 down	6 across 10 down	3 across 5 down	8 yards	8 yards

Figure 12

Fabric for a Pieced Top

Look at one square. Determine roughly what proportion of each color is in that square. Example: ½ blue, ¼ white, ¼ yellow. If your total top requires 6 yards of fabric, buy 3 yards (½) blue, 1½ yards (¼) white, and 1½ yards (¼) yellow.

Armed with all the facts and figures, head for a fabric store. Don't forget to buy the batting.

Patchwork and appliqué quilts—cut top and back squares. Piecework quilts—cut only back squares (the tops are made up of pieces of fabric sewn together).

Reach for scissors, ruler, pencil, and pins. You are ready to attack your washed, dried, and pressed fabrics. Cut all the squares, following the easy cutting guide you have chosen.

Cutting Guide Using Small Back Squares

1. Make a cardboard pattern the size of the top square you are using.

2. Make a cardboard pattern ½ inch larger for the back square.

3. Cut the back squares first, using the common lines.

4. Don't cut the shaded area (*Figure 13*); save it for the strips.

5. Cut the batting squares the same size as the top squares.

Cutting Guide Using Large Back Squares

1. Make a cardboard pattern the size of the top square you are using.

2. Using a tape measure, mark a back square the size of four top squares. Use this as a pattern to cut the rest of the back squares. Cut on common lines.

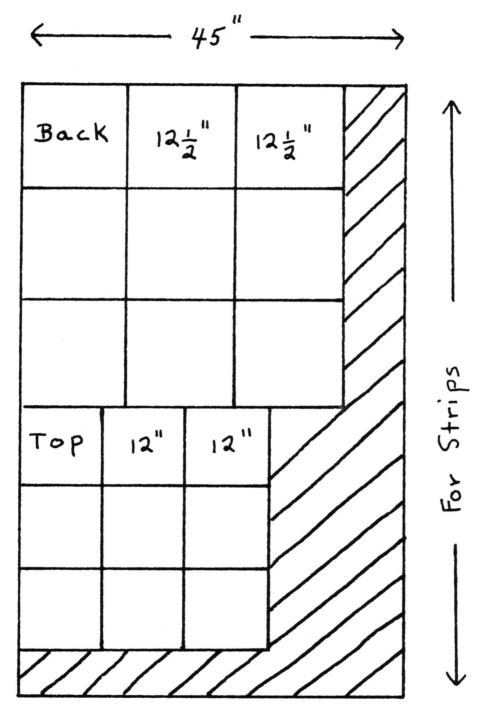

Figure 13

3. Cut the back squares first.

4. Don't cut the shaded area (*Figure 14*); save it for the strips or borders.

5. Cut the batting squares the same size as the large back square.

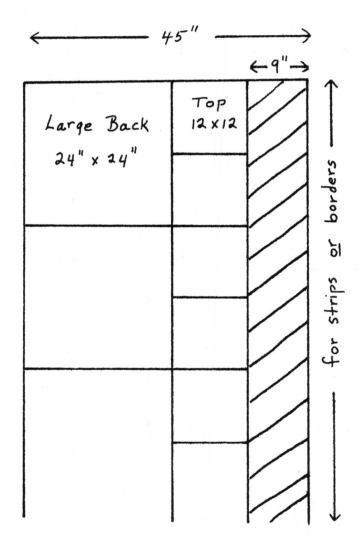

Figure 14

FOR MATH MAJORS

How to Determine Measurements

1. Know the mattress size of the bed.

2. Decide how much the quilt will hang over the sides of the bed (*Figure 7*).

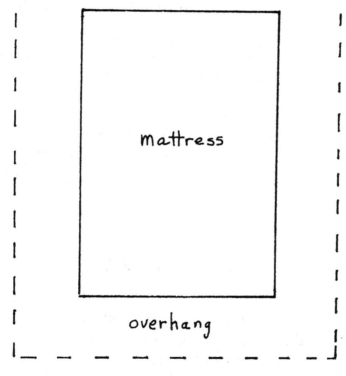

Figure 7

3. Determine the actual size of the quilt, using the formula below:

OVERHANG + MATTRESS WIDTH + OVERHANG = QUILT *WIDTH.*

MATTRESS LENGTH + OVERHANG = QUILT *LENGTH.*

4. *For the quilt top*: Decide on the size square (block) that best fits into the measurements. (This may change the overall quilt size by a few inches.) First divide the square size into the width measurement. This gives you the number of squares going *across* the quilt. Then divide the square size into the length measurement to determine the number of squares in the quilt's *length*. Multiply the two together to find out the total number of squares in the quilt top.

   For the quilt back: If you are using *small* back squares you will need the same number of squares as the top but they must be ½ inch larger.

   For large back squares: Divide the number of top squares by 4 and this gives you the number you need.

5. Write down the quilt measurements. Write down the number of top squares and the number of back squares you will need. With these numbers figure out the yards of fabric you will need to buy.

FIGURE THE FABRIC

If Your Quilt Has Small Top and Back Squares

   Using the number of squares in the quilt back, figure out how many squares will fit across the *width* of 45-inch fabric. Divide this number into the total number of squares in the quilt back. This tells you how many *rows* of squares you will need going down the *length* of the fabric. Now take this same number of rows and multiply it by the size of your square. This will give you the number of inches you need for the *back*. Convert this to yards.

   For the top squares: Proceed exactly the same way. Then add the yardage for the top and back together, and ½ YARD EXTRA FOR GOOD MEASURE! Check *Figure 15* for converting inches to yards.

   Cut the squares, using the cutting guide for small back squares in *Figure 13*.

If Your Quilt Has Large Back Squares

For the Back Squares

Take the number of large back squares you need and figure out how many will fit across 45-inch fabric (it is usually only one). Divide this number into the total number of large squares in the quilt back. This tells you how many *rows* of squares you will need going down the *length* of the fabric. Now take this same number of rows and multiply it by the size of your large square. This will give you the number of inches you need for the back squares. Convert this to yards.

HELPFUL CHART FOR CONVERTING INCHES TO YARDS

36 inches	=	1 yard
72 ″	=	2 yards
108 ″	=	3 ″
144 ″	=	4 ″
180 ″	=	5 ″
216 ″	=	6 ″
252 ″	=	7 ″
288 ″	=	8 ″
324 ″	=	9 ″
360 ″	= 10 ″
396 ″	= 11 ″
432 ″	= 12 ″

Figure 15

For the Top Squares

You can see from *Figure 14* that there is room for two top squares beside each large back square. This will take care of half the total number of top squares you need. Figure out how many of the remaining top squares will fit across 45-inch fabric. Divide this number into the top squares still needed. This tells you how many *rows* of squares you'll need going down the *length* of the fabric. Now take this same number of rows and multiply it by the size of your square. This will give you the number of inches needed for the rest of the top squares. Convert to yards and add all the yardage together, plus ½ YARD EXTRA FOR GOOD MEASURE! Check *Figure 15* for converting inches to yards.

Cut the squares, using the cutting guide for large back squares in *Figure 14*.

This is the cutting guide we suggest you use if your are planning borders. Nine-inch borders can be cut from the shaded area.

BE A NEAT-NIC

Collect the supplies and materials you need.

Quilting thread comes in white and colors. It is waxed so it will slide through the three layers easily. It also doesn't tangle, so use it for all sewing.

Batting comes in sizes from crib to queen (for king you need two twin packages). It also comes in various thicknesses. Avoid "super fluff" unless you are making a tied quilt.

A word to the wise: quilt all the blocks in the same color so the back of the quilt looks as lovely as the front. Quilting needles are short and sharp. Use these or regular sewing needles.

Stop, pause, and *think*—then cut the squares and patterns.

Stuff everything needed for each square in a plastic bag and carry it around with you. Friends will wonder if you are pulling out a sandwich or your sewing!

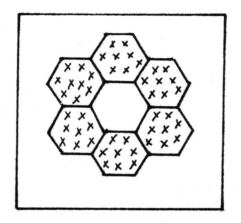

1
PATCHWORK
▼▛▜▛▜▛▜▛▜▛▜▛▀

FIRST THINGS FIRST—
A HEXAGON SQUARE IS THE EASIEST TO LEARN

"Grandmother's Flower Garden," which is made up of hexagons, was a very popular quilt pattern in this country. Paper liners were used to aid in the construction. Often these paper liners were left sewn in the quilts to provide added warmth; they are also one of the ways by which we have been able to date antique quilts.

This is one 12-inch x 12-inch hexagon square (*Figure 16*). Let's make it!

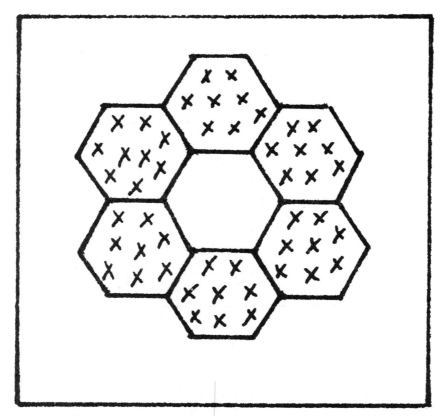

Figure 16

Trace the hexagon (*Figure 17*) very accurately onto tracing paper. Transfer it to shirt cardboard, using a ruler and carbon paper. Cut the cardboard hexagon out on the line. This is a pattern, called a template. In order to make accurate fabric hexagons you need to cut paper liners. To do this place the cardboard hexagon template on top of not more than two thicknesses of magazine paper. Draw

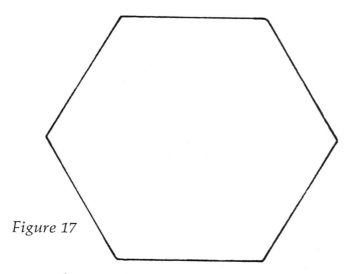

Figure 17

around the template and cut on the line. Six paper liners make up a circle of hexagons (seven if you would like a hexagon in the center). Set the paper liners aside and take out the pretty prints you are using for the hexagons (you may want to use a plain color, too).

Place the cardboard template on the *wrong* side of the fabric on the straight of the goods. Hexagon *A* (*Figure 18*) is placed correctly with two of its sides running with the straight; *B* is incorrect.

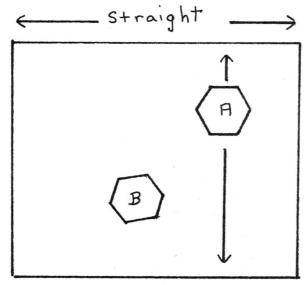

Figure 18

Draw around the template with a pencil. Then draw five more hexagons, allowing ¼-inch seam allowance around each. Cut each hexagon out, cutting ¼-inch seam allowance by eye (*Figure 19*). (The line will scream at you to cut on it, but don't! Cut ¼ inch away from it.)

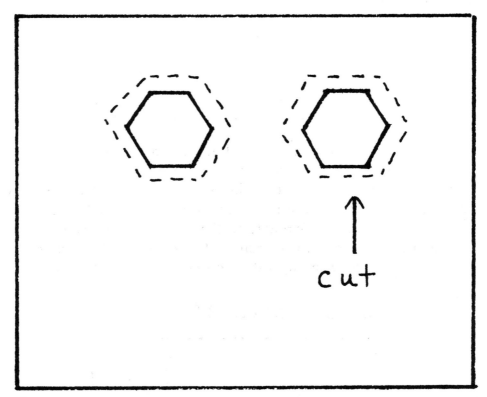

Figure 19

Pin a paper liner on the wrong side of each fabric hexagon. Fold fabric edges over and baste down into the paper, neatly folding the corners over (*Figure 20*).

Join the hexagons as follows: Pin two hexagons right sides together. Using matching single thread, hide the knot in the fold. Sew as in *Figure 21*, catching each edge with small stitches. This stitch is called the whipping stitch. Join three hexagons together first, then

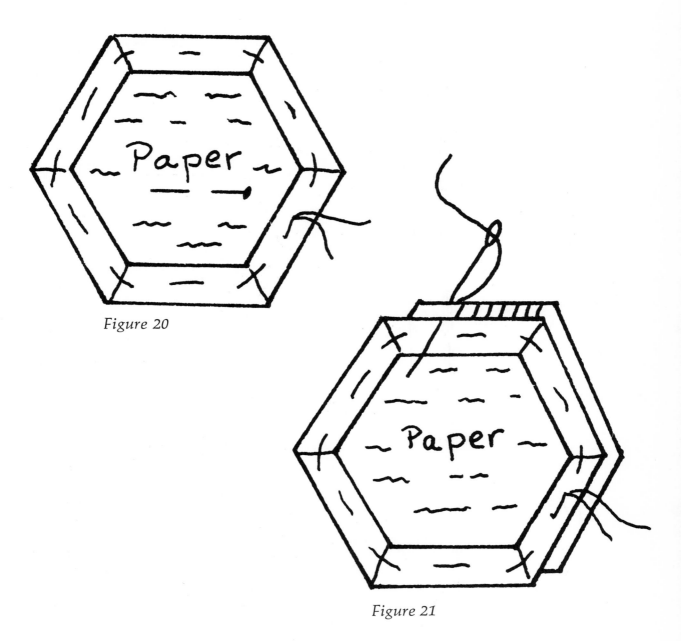

Figure 20

Figure 21

join the other three. Now join the two sections, using the same whipping stitch (*Figure 22*). Press the hexagon circle, papers and all. The time to remove the papers and bastings is now (unless this quilt is for your unheated cottage!).

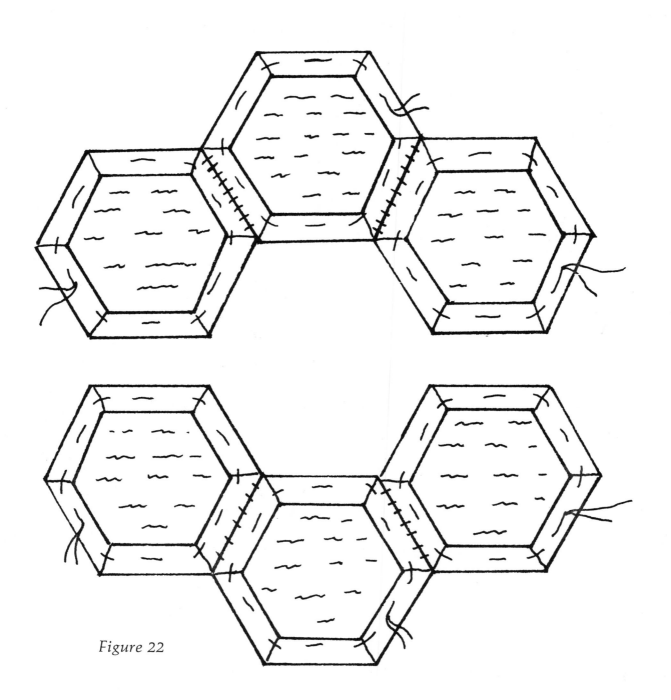

Figure 22

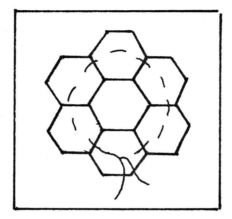

Figure 23

Pin and baste the hexagon circle to the center of a top square (*Figure 23*). Stitch it down as follows: Knot the thread and come up from underneath into the fold. Go down directly opposite where you came up originally. Continue going forward; the stitches are about ¼ inch apart. The stitches on the right side will not show if your up-and-down stitches are directly opposite each other (*Figure 24*). This stitch is called the blind stitch. It is used to anchor the patchwork to a piece of fabric, in this case the top square. When you are finished sewing, give it a good press, step back, and take a look —aren't you pleased?

Figure 24

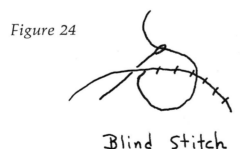

Blind Stitch

IT'S QUILTING TIME!

The purpose of quilting is to hold the three layers together: the top, the batting, and the back (the back square is the underside of a quilt block, sometimes called the "backing" square). The three layers are put together like a sandwich.

Place the backing square on a table wrong side up, and lay the batting square on top of it. Then put the hexagon square on top of both, right side up. Pin the three layers together and baste from the center out, having the knots on the top for easy removal (*Figure 25*).

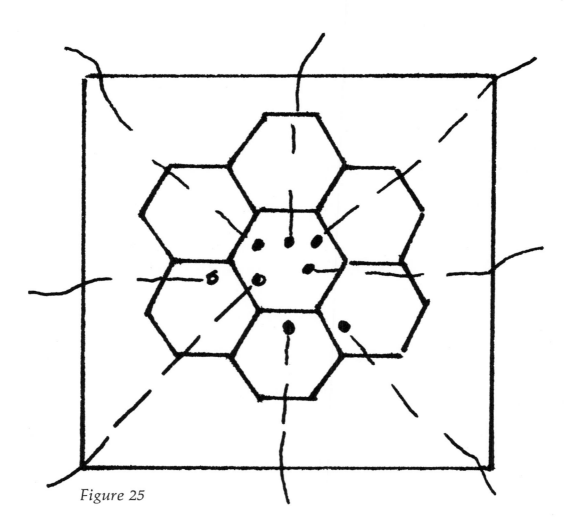

Figure 25

How to Quilt

The quilting stitch is a small running stitch going down through all three layers: the top, the batting, and the backing. It is evenly spaced and evenly stitched. Generally you should have five to seven stitches to the inch, but don't get into a panic if they don't

Figure 26

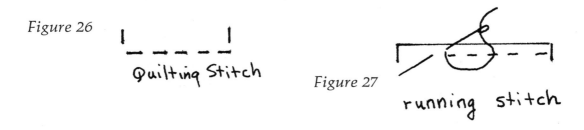

Figure 27

Figure 28a

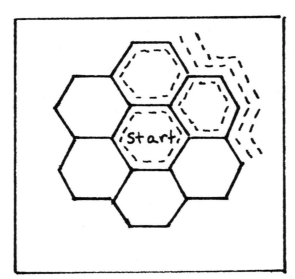

measure up. Go for even stitches, not the tiny, tiny ones (*Figures 26, 27*).

Thread a needle with a single piece of quilting thread. Make a *small* knot, snip off the tail, and put your thimble on the third finger of your hand. Start by coming up from underneath at the center-most point (*Figure 28a*). Give a quick pull, losing the knot in the batting—it makes a clicking sound. (Pulling the backing square away makes it easier for the knot to slip through.) Go straight down through all three layers, touching your finger, and then come up to the top, making a small stitch. (Touching your finger ensures that you have gone through the three layers.) Take two, three, or four stitches on the needle and then draw through. Never mind if your finger gets sore—it will develop a callus very quickly and the fun and beauty of quilting far surpasses a slightly worn-looking finger!

To end the thread off, go down to the underside of the backing square and take a stitch, going through the backing square and catching some batting. Then take another stitch right over the previous stitch. Now run the needle off to the side through the batting, pull the fabric up a little, and snip off the thread. The end is lost between the layers.

The amount of quilting you do is a matter of personal preference. It is most important to quilt from the center of the square toward the edges. This prevents the batting from bunching up in the center. The stitches will become even with practice. Don't pull them too tightly; let them flow. A very important point to remember: don't quilt any closer to the edge of the square than a good ½ inch. You will need the ½ inch of unquilted fabric when you join the square to another square as you put the quilt together. (More than ½ inch of unquilted fabric around the edge makes the whole process even easier!)

You have made "Grandmother's Square." Turn it over—the back is beautiful *(Figure 28b)*!

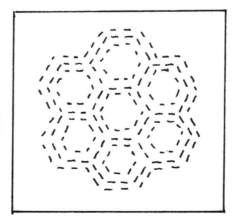

Figure 28 b

Figure 29

ANOTHER PATCHWORK PATTERN—MAYBE DIAMONDS ARE FOR YOU!

Star quilts lead the list of American patterns. "Twinkling Star," "Shooting Star," "Star of Bethlehem," and "Texas Star" are some of the many names given these gorgeous quilts. They are made exactly like the hexagon quilts but the pattern is a diamond.

Let's make a diamond square. It's very much the same as a circle of hexagons. All the steps are the same except for making the diamond. Follow the easy diagrams. This is one 12-inch x 12-inch diamond square (*Figure 29*). Look at it and plan your fabrics.

Accuracy is most important! Trace the diamond in *Figure 30.* Make a cardboard template and eight paper liners (eight diamonds make up a circle).

Place the cardboard template on the *wrong* side of the fabric so that two sides of the diamond are on the straight of the goods. Diamond *A* (*Figure 31*) is placed correctly with two sides running with the straight; *B* is incorrect. Cut the ¼-inch seam allowance by eye—remember, *not* on the line (*Figure 32*)!

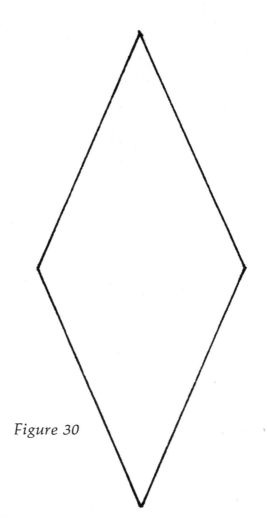

Figure 30

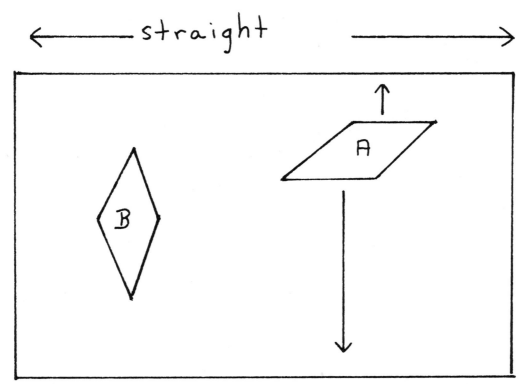

Figure 31

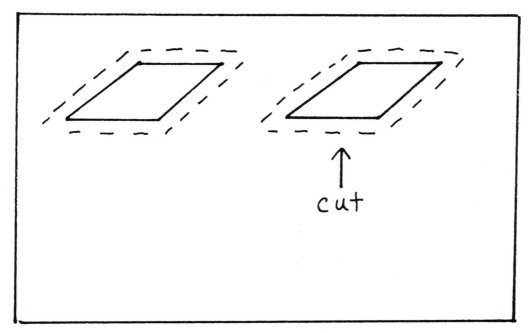

Figure 32

Pin the paper liners to the wrong side of the diamonds and fold the edges over. Points *A* and *B* are folded the same way as the hexagons. Points *C* and *D* are folded differently in order to make sharp points. Knowing how to make these sharp points is one of the tricks in sewing. Fold the fabric over point *C*, and then fold each side in and baste around the edges (*Figures 33, 34*).

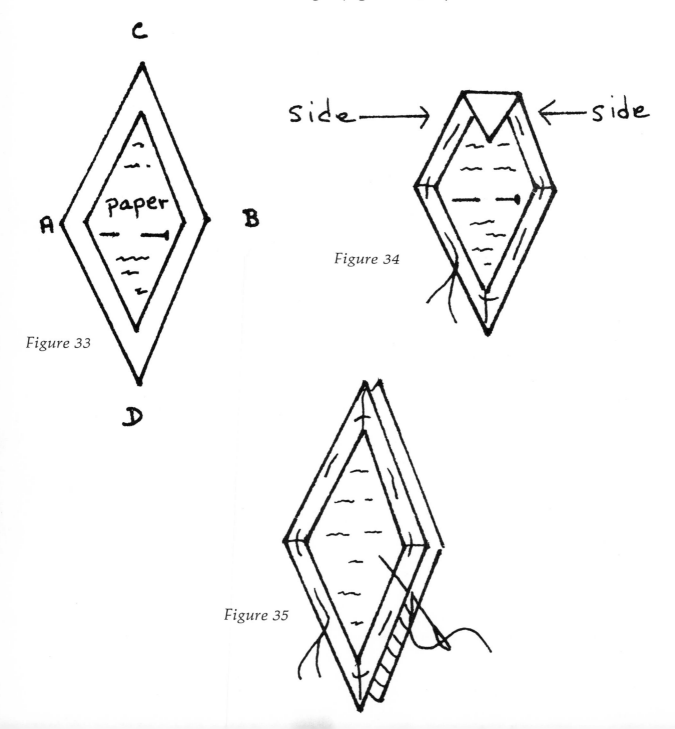

Figure 33

Figure 34

Figure 35

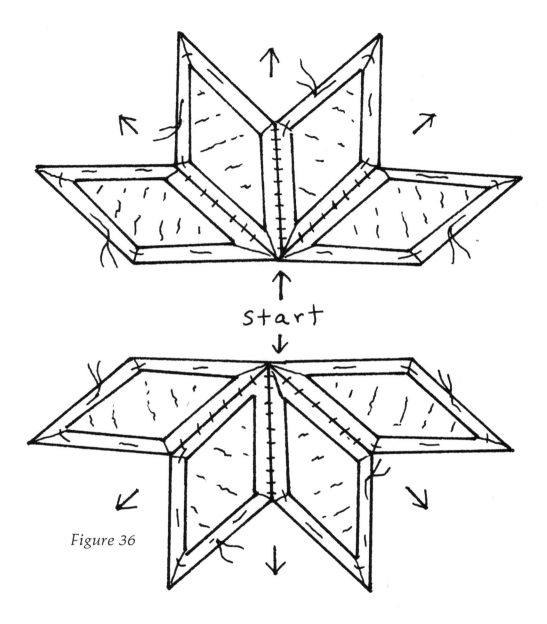

Figure 36

Join the diamonds, using the whipping stitch. Whip four diamonds together first, then the other four, and then join both sections. Start at the point that will be the center of the star (*Figures
35, 36*).

Press the finished star of diamonds and remove the papers and
bastings.

Center the star on a top square; pin and baste it down.

When the blind stitching is finished, give the square a good press. Quilt it the same way as the hexagon and see how pretty it looks (*Figure 37*).

"Twinkling Star," "Morning Star," "Shooting Star," and yours—the "Square Star"! Learn to put all those star blocks together by turning to Chapter 4, "Building Blocks into Quilts."

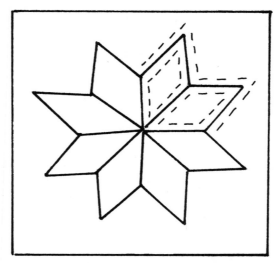

Figure 37

2
APPLIQUÉ

Wreath of Roses," "Basket of Flowers," pineapples, tulips, trees, "Sunbonnet Sue," "Buffalo Bill," "Spot the Dog," and the "Calico Cat"—all and anything lends itself to appliqué. Perhaps the marriage quilts are the most famous of the traditional patterns. A bride-to-be was given squares made by her family and friends. Each square was an appliquéd picture symbolic of life. Almost always a heart was found somewhere on the quilt. You don't necessarily have to be an artist to do appliqué. Patterns can be found in books and catalogs. A child's coloring book with simple line drawings is a wonderful source of patterns. Whether you use a ready-made pattern or create one, it will be all yours because of the fabric *you* have picked to use. See Plates 21 and 22.

"SUNBONNET SUE"

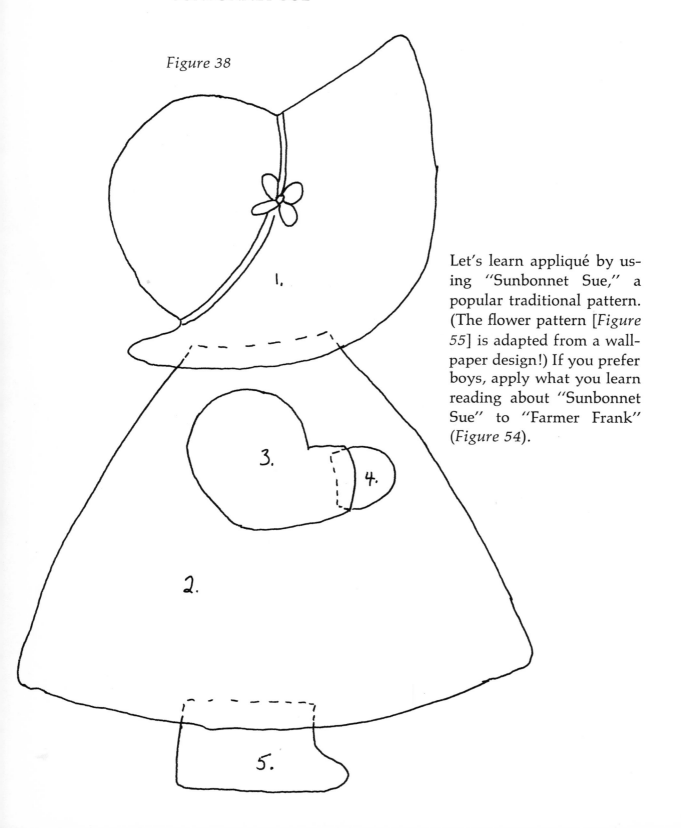

Figure 38

Let's learn appliqué by using "Sunbonnet Sue," a popular traditional pattern. (The flower pattern [*Figure 55*] is adapted from a wallpaper design!) If you prefer boys, apply what you learn reading about "Sunbonnet Sue" to "Farmer Frank" (*Figure 54*).

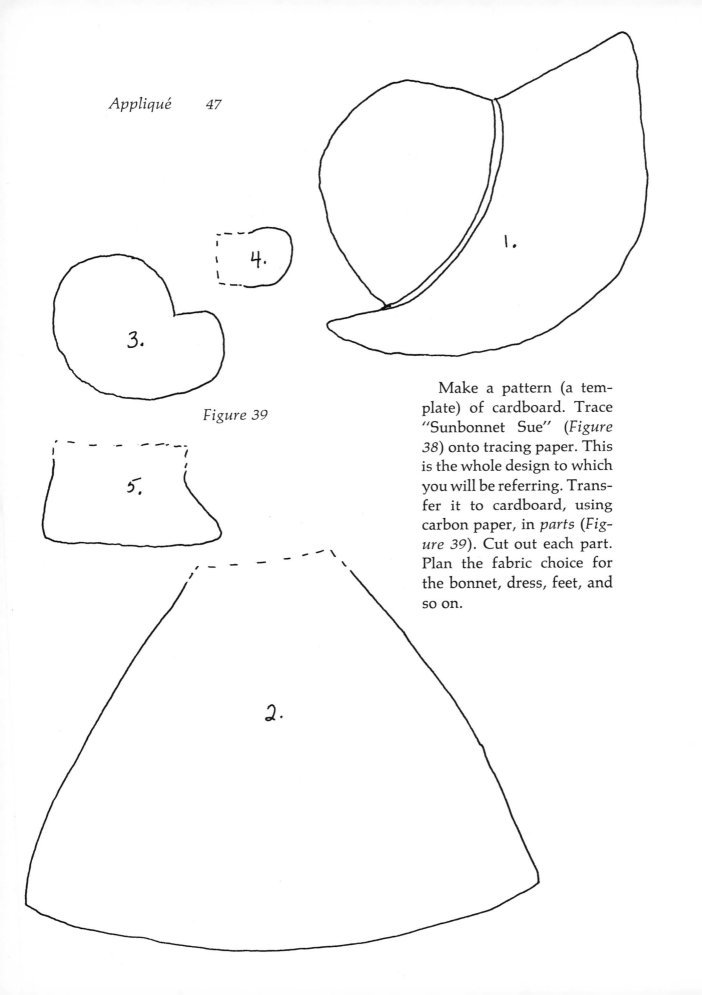

Figure 39

Make a pattern (a template) of cardboard. Trace "Sunbonnet Sue" (*Figure 38*) onto tracing paper. This is the whole design to which you will be referring. Transfer it to cardboard, using carbon paper, in *parts* (*Figure 39*). Cut out each part. Plan the fabric choice for the bonnet, dress, feet, and so on.

Place the template parts on the *right* side of the fabric, not too close together, and mark with a pencil just dark enough to see. Cut the parts out, leaving ¼-inch seam allowance by eye around each section. Extend the parts that go under—for example, the hand has to fit under the dress sleeve, the shoes under the dress (*Figure 40*).

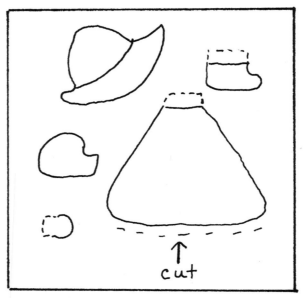

Figure 40

In order to make the appliqué lie flat you must clip the curves and V's. Snip to the seam line (*Figure 41*).

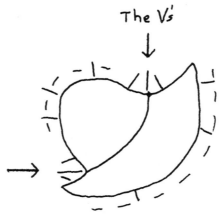

Figure 41

Here is a trick to help you make sharp points on the bonnet (use it in future sewing projects!):

1. Fold point *A* over.

2. Then fold each side in (*Figures 42, 43, 44*).

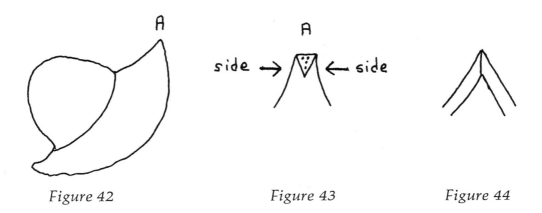

Figure 42   Figure 43   Figure 44

Set Her on Top

Pin or baste "Sunbonnet Sue" in place on a top square, referring to the original drawing (*Figure 45*).

Figure 45

Thread your needle with matching single thread and prepare to sew her down. Turn the edges under on the pencil line. It is not necessary to pin or baste before you sew, as working with the needle and one or two pins is satisfactory. Remember—no need to turn the top of the shoes in, because they fit under the dress.

Blind stitch as follows: Knot the thread and come up from underneath into the fold. Go down directly opposite where you came up originally. Continue going forward; the stitches are about ¼ inch apart. The stitches on the right side will not show if your up-and-down stitches are directly opposite each other. This stitch is used to anchor the appliqué. It is quite invisible (*Figure 46*).

Figure 46

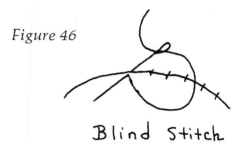

Blind Stitch

Decorate "Sue" with Embroidery

Put a bow on her bonnet, a flower in her hand, or add trim to her dress. Embroidery on appliqué is like icing on a cake. Use two or three strands of embroidery floss.

Stem Stitch (Figure 47)

1. Needle comes up at *a*, down at *b*, up at *c*, which is halfway between *a* and *b*. Draw through, holding thread *either* above or below the needle.

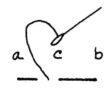

Figure 47a

2. Needle goes down at *d* and up at *b* in the same hole made previously.

Continue going forward, always being sure to hold the thread on the same side of needle (either above or below).

Figure 47 b

Split Stitch (Figure 48)

Thread comes up at *a*, down at *b*, and up at *c* halfway between *a* and *b* and splits the stitch exactly in the middle.

Figure 48

Arrow Head (Figure 49)

Needle comes up at *a*, down at *b*, up at *c*, down at *a*, up at *d*, and down at *a*. Continue going forward.

"Sunbonnet Sue" is finished—just iron out her wrinkles.

Figure 49

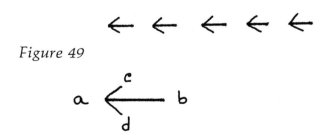

START QUILTING

The purpose of quilting is to hold the three layers together: the top, the batting, and the back (the back square is the underside of a quilt block, sometimes called the "backing square"). Stack, then baste the layers—the backing, batting, and top square—together like a sandwich.

Baste the appliqué square (*Figure 50*).

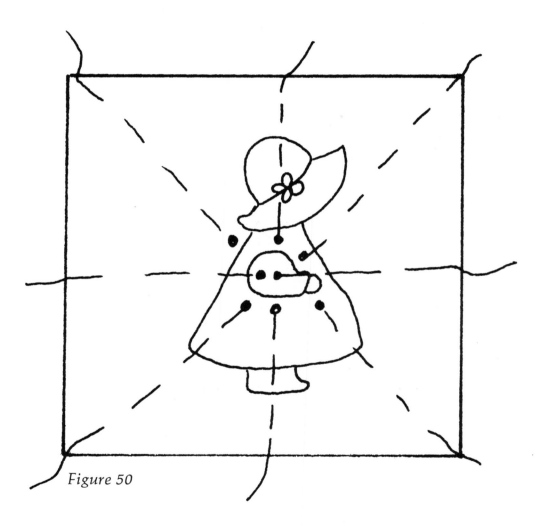

Figure 50

How to Quilt

The quilting stitch is a small running stitch going down through all three layers: the top, the batting, and the backing. It is evenly spaced and evenly stitched (*Figures 51, 52*). Generally you should have five to seven stitches to the inch, but don't worry if you don't—you should improve with practice.

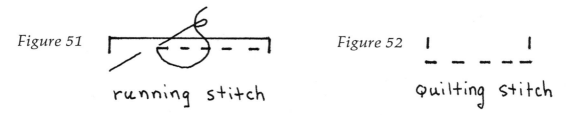

Figure 51   running stitch   Figure 52   quilting stitch

Thread a needle with a single piece of quilting thread. Make a small knot, snip off the tail, and put your thimble on the third finger of your hand. Start by coming up from underneath at the center-most point (*Figure 53*). Give a quick pull, losing the knot in the batting—it makes a clicking sound. (This may take some practice. Pulling the backing square away makes it easier for the knot to slip through.) Go straight through all three layers, touching your finger, and then come up to the top, making a small stitch. (Touching your finger ensures that you have gone through the three layers.) Take

Figure 53

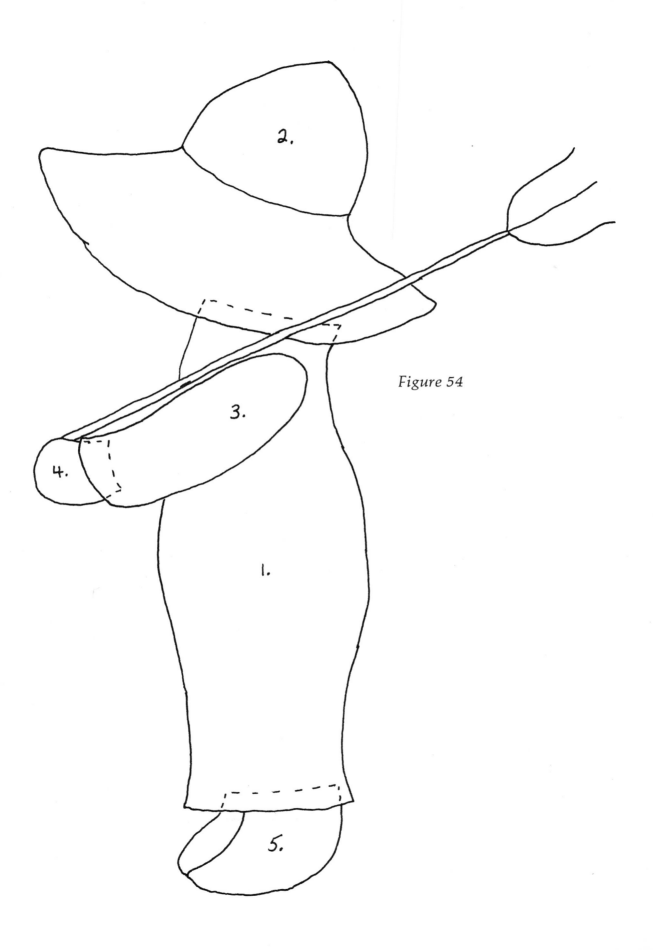

Figure 54

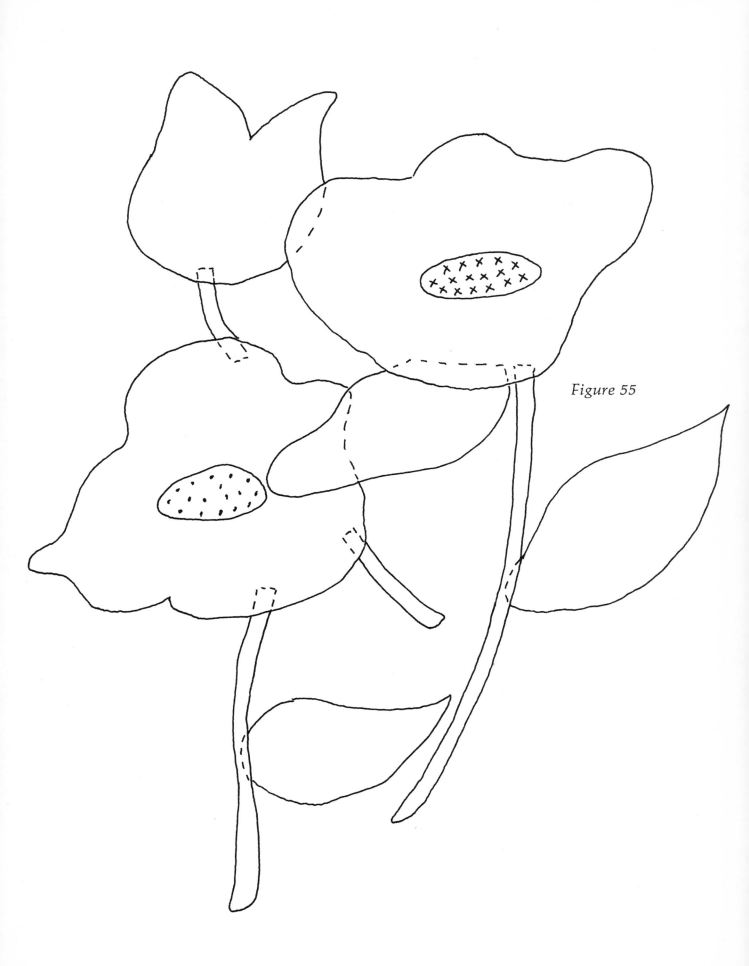

Figure 55

two, three, or four stitches on the needle and then draw through. If your finger gets sore, wrap a piece of adhesive tape around it. This helps!

To end the thread off, go down to the underside of the backing square and take a stitch, going through the backing square and catching some batting. Then take another stitch right over the previous stitch. Now run the needle off to the side through the batting, pull the fabric up a little, and snip the thread off. The end is lost between the layers.

The amount of quilting you do is a matter of personal preference. It is most important to quilt from the center of the square toward the edges. This prevents the batting from bunching up in the center. Don't pull the stitches too tightly; let them flow. A very important point to remember: don't quilt any closer to the edge of the square than a good ½ inch. You will need the ½ inch of unquilted fabric when you join the square to another square when you put the quilt together. (More than ½ inch of unquilted fabric around the edge makes the whole process even easier!)

A square a day—speeds you on your way.

Other patterns for appliqué: *Figures 54, 55* (pages 54 and 55).

QUILTING DESIGNS

Squares can be made up with quilting designs. These designs are quilted in the outline of any appliqué, patchwork, or pieced pattern.

"Sue"—the Quilt Design

Transfer "Sue" to manila paper with the aid of carbon paper. With a ripper or small sharp scissors, poke holes on all the lines ¼ inch or more apart, and on all the intersections (*Figure 56*). Mark a plain top square with a T (to indicate the top of the square). Place

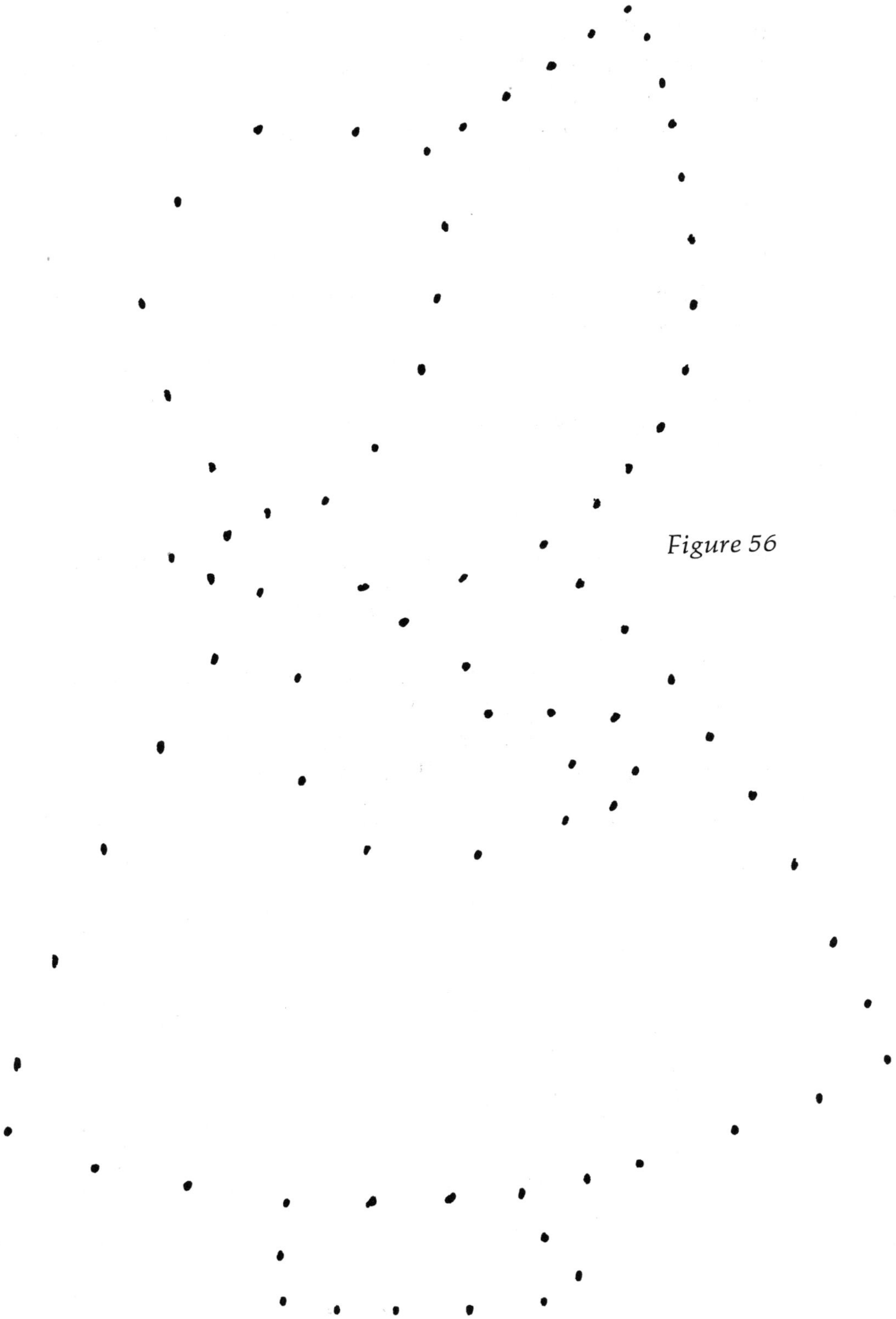

Figure 56

the shot-full-of-holes "Sunbonnet Sue" on the right side of the fabric and hold her down. Lightly twist a pencil in all the holes, making dots only dark enough to see.

"Sue" is then stacked: backing, batting, and the top square.

Baste from the center out to edges.

Dot to Dot

Starting at the centermost point quilt from dot to dot, being sure to go through the three layers. Don't end the thread unnecessarily; run it through the batting if you want to get to another section.

Appliquéd "Sue" and plain "Sue" look very well together in a quilt.

PATCHWORK AND PIECEWORK QUILTING DESIGNS

A square may be quilted with plain lines. These lines are called grids.

Grids are made by placing a ruler down on the right side of the fabric. Mark dots along the edge, flip the ruler over, and continue marking dots. Quilt from dot to dot and from the center out to within ½ inch of the edges (*Figures 57, 58, 59*).

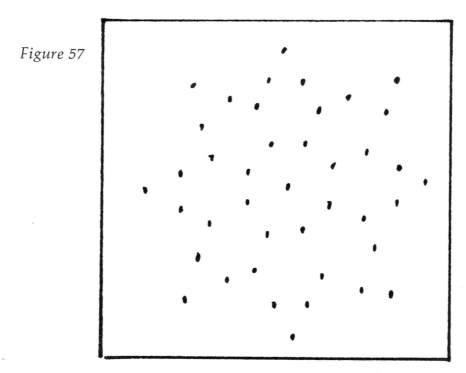

Figure 57

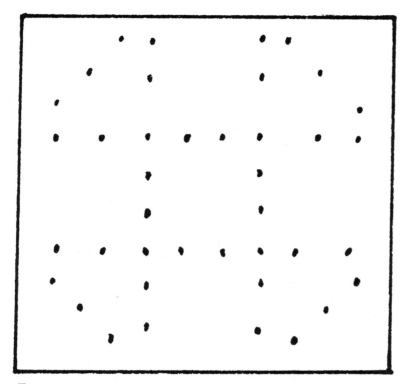

Figure 58

Figure 59

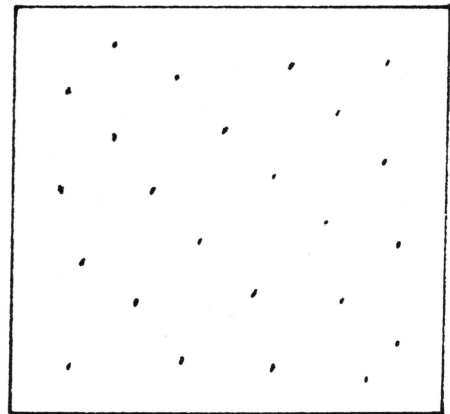

Figure 60

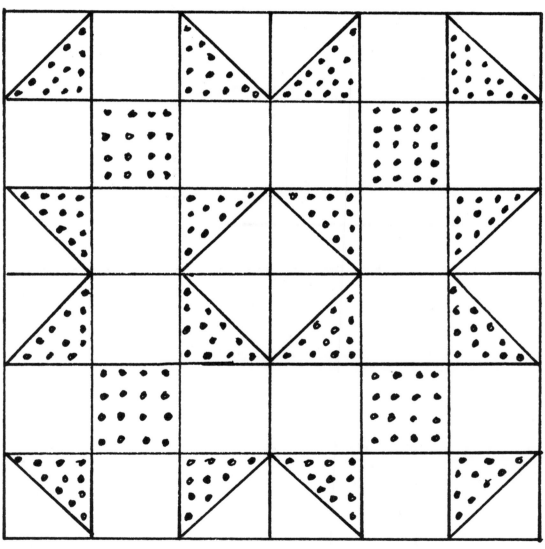

four squares joined together

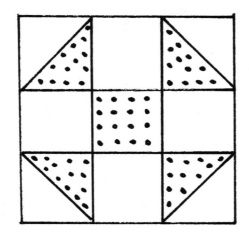

3
PIECEWORK

Have you ever marveled at "Log Cabin," "Babies' Blocks," "Monkey Wrench," "Bow Tie"? These old-time traditional patterns are made up of small pieces of fabric sewn together, and they may in turn make up another overall geometrical design (*Figure 60*). See Plate 19.

Figure 61 is made up of triangles and squares. Make two sets of cardboard patterns (templates). One set will include the ¼-inch seam allowance needed for sewing the pieces together. The other set will be the actual size of the pattern. With both sets the block will be accurate, which is most important in piecework!

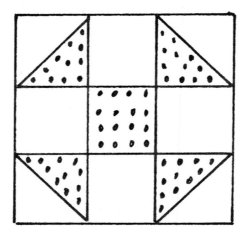

Figure 61

First make the actual-size set of templates. Using the corners and edges of a shirt cardboard, mark off two 4-inch squares (*Figure 62*). Cut out both squares; cut one in half, making two triangles (discard one). These are your actual-size templates: one square and one triangle.

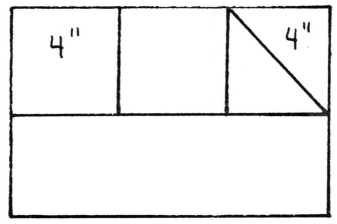

Figure 62

Now make the larger templates, which include the ¼-inch seam allowance needed for sewing the pieces together. Using the corners and edges of another shirt cardboard, mark off and cut one 4½-inch square on the left-hand side as in *Figure 63*. You now have one square 4½ inches x 4½ inches, which includes the ¼-inch seam allowance on all four sides. You can see this by placing the actual-size 4-inch square on top.

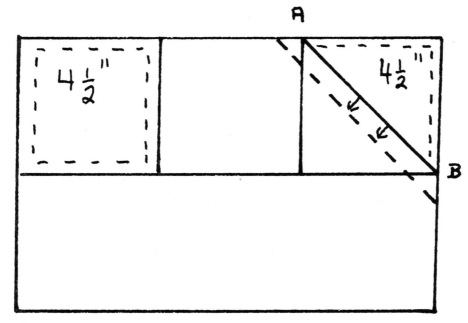

Figure 63

Draw a second 4½-inch square in the right-hand corner. Draw a straight line from *A* to *B* as in *Figure 63*, dividing the square into two triangles. The outside triangle already has the ¼-inch seam allowance on two edges. Take your ruler and add ¼ inch along line *A–B* indicated by the arrows. Cut on the broken line. You now have a 4½-inch triangle which includes the seam allowance on all three sides. You can see this by placing the 4-inch actual-size triangle on top.

Set the smaller set of templates aside. The *larger* ones are used for cutting the fabric.

PRINTS AND PLAINS—FOR SQUARES AND TRIANGLES

You will cut (*Figure 64*):

4 print triangles
4 plain triangles
1 print square
4 plain squares

If any of the fabrics are dark, a white dressmaker pencil is a must.

(*Text continues on page 81.*)

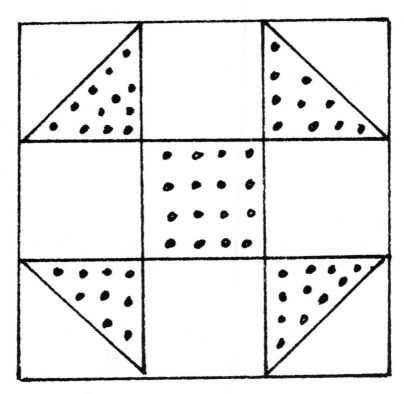

Figure 64

Plate 1.
Betty's patchwork star quilt for her antique bed—four top squares joined together on a large back square.

Plate 2.
Kappy's pieced quilt called "Connecticut"—four top squares joined together on a large back square.

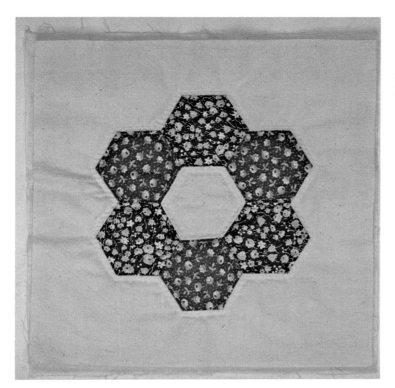

Plate 3.
Hexagon square—patchwork.

Plate 4.
Star—patchwork.

Plate 5.
Wallpaper flowers—
appliqué.

Plate 6.
"Sunbonnet Sue"—
appliqué.

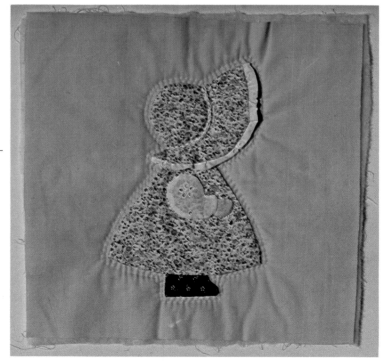

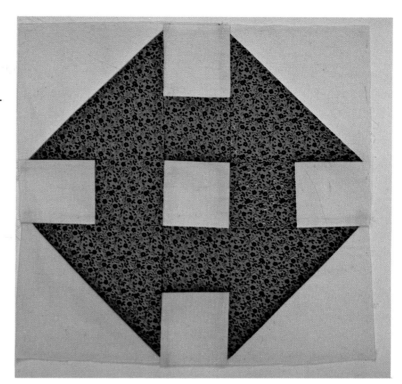

Plate 7.
Piecework.

Plate 8.
Wall-hanging sampler with "Farmer Frank."

Plate 9.
Tied quilt—names embroidered on a square by some of our students.

Plate 10.
"The Wrench"—piecework tied quilt for a bassinet by Betty.

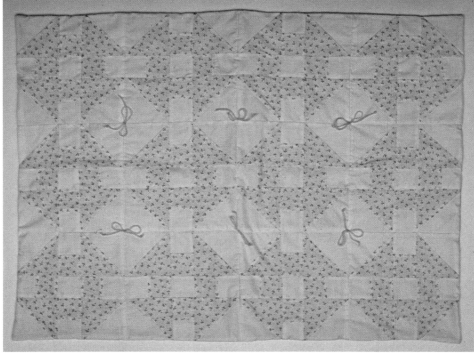

Plate 11.
The class sampler.

Plate 12.
Biscuits.

Plate 13.
"Cathedral Window."

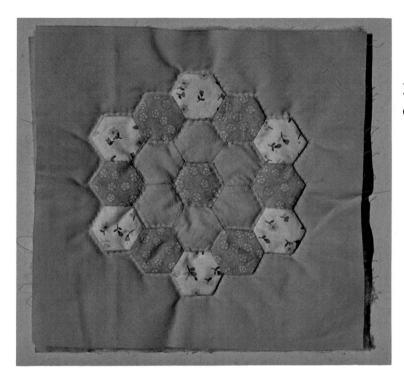

Plate 14.
"Grandmother's Flower
Garden."

Plate 15.
"Parade Hill Farm"—wall hang-
ing; a combination of piecework,
appliqué, and embroidery by
Kappy.

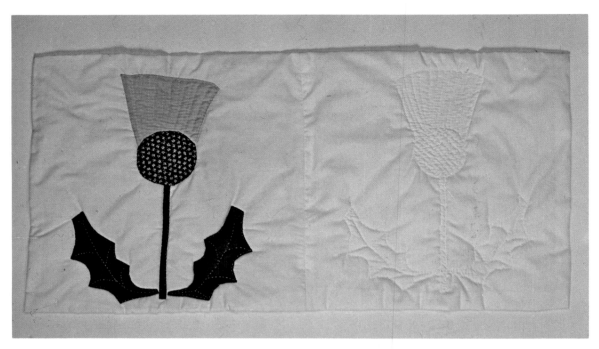

Plate 16.
Appliqué thistle and plain quilting.

Plate 17.
"Friendship" or "Dresden Plate" carriage quilt—patchwork.

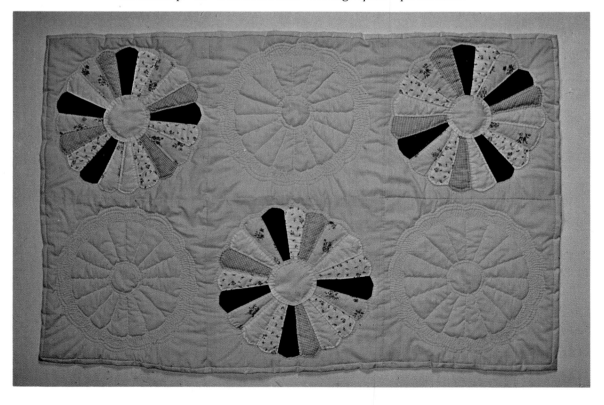

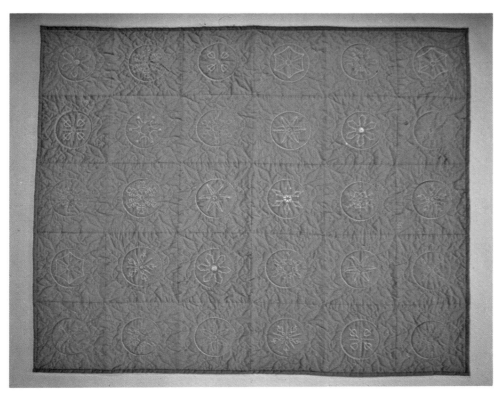

Plate 18.
Snowflake embroidered quilt by the authors and some of the members of New Canaan Sewing Group B.

Plate 19.
"Log Cabin"—a pieced quilt made for a sleigh bed by Kappy.

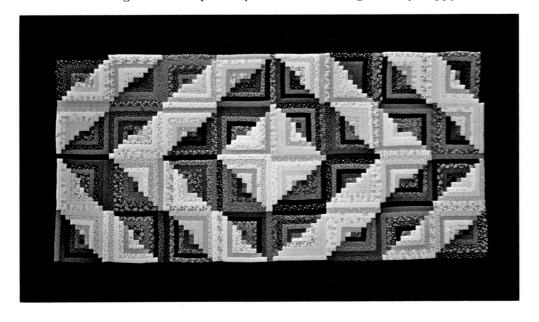

Plate 20.
"New Canaan Bicentennial" quilt—appliquéd scenes from our town; designed
by Ann Price and made by the New Canaan Quilters.

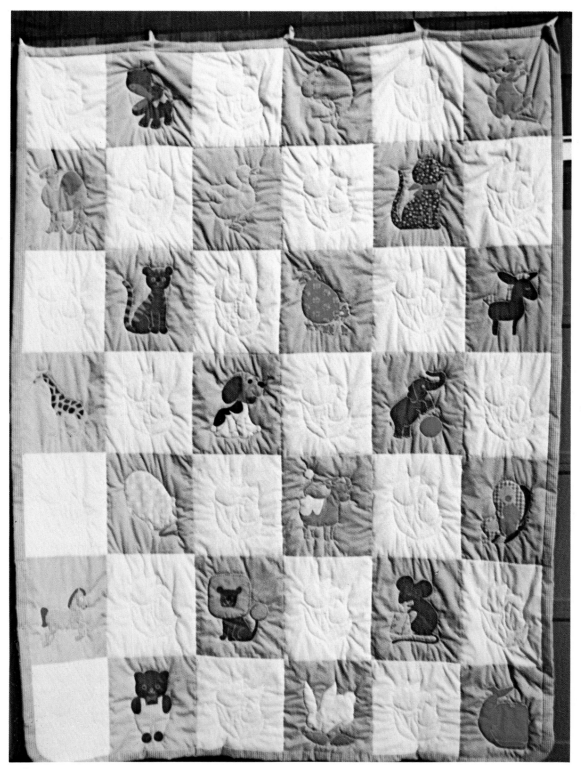

Plate 21.
Quilt for Sara by grandmother, Lois Harman (detail, Plate 22).

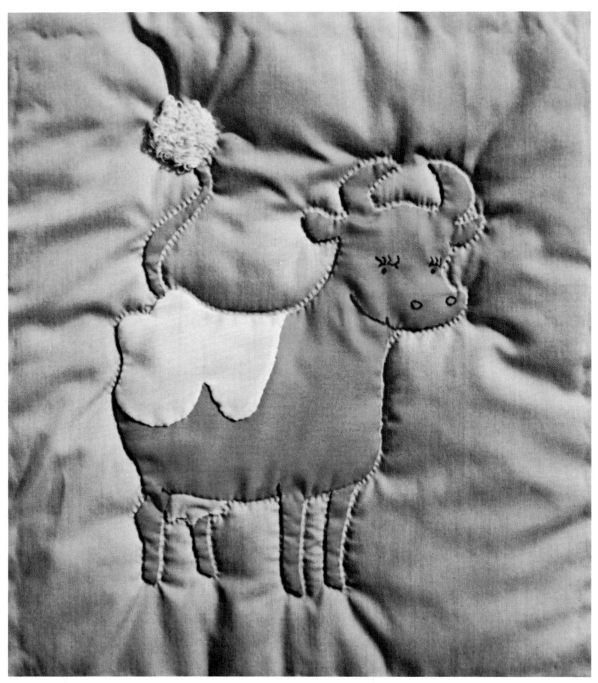

Plate 22.
Close-up of cow in Sara's quilt.

Plate 23.
Nancy Ryan's patch pieced pattern quilt.

Plate 24.
"Wreath of Roses"—traditional appliqué pattern by the authors.

CUTTING UP

Place the 4½-inch square on the wrong side of the print fabric and mark around with a pencil. Place the 4½-inch triangle on the *wrong* side of the print fabric and draw around it. Flip it over, making another triangle. Use line *A–B* as the common line (*Figure 65*).

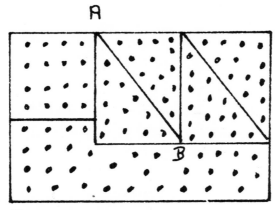

Figure 65

Place the 4½-inch square on the wrong side of the plain fabric, making four squares. Place the 4½-inch triangle on the *wrong* side of the plain fabric, making four triangles. Flip them over on common line *A–B* (*Figure 66*).

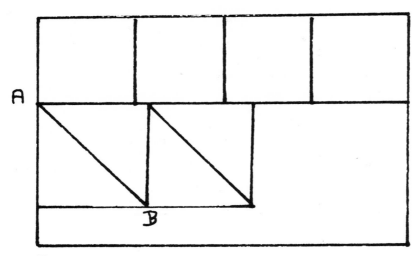

Figure 66

Using 4-inch actual-size templates make marks on the plain fabric *only*, as in *Figure 67*, to indicate the seam allowance. These marks are the guide lines for sewing.

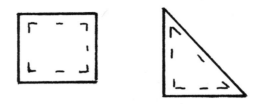

Figure 67

Cut out pieces on the solid lines and lay them in front of you, right side up, in their proper place (*Figure 68*).

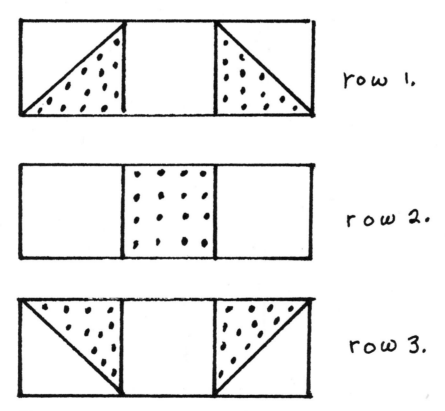

Figure 68

Piecework is always sewn together by rows. Starting with row 1, first join plain and print triangles. You do this by placing right sides together. Pin and sew across the seam on guide lines, using single thread and a running stitch (*Figure 69*). Triangles should be pressed, placing seam allowance to one side—this makes a stronger seam (do not open the seam). Snip the fabric tails off (*Figure 70*).

Figure 69

running stitch

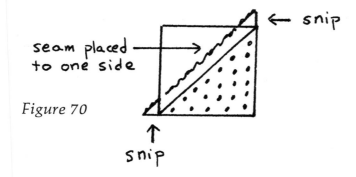

seam placed to one side →

← snip

Figure 70

↑ snip

Sew the three parts of row 1 together. When you join the square to a triangle-made-square it will look like *Figure 71*. The distance between *A* and *B* is ¼ inch and will be taken up when you

Figure 71

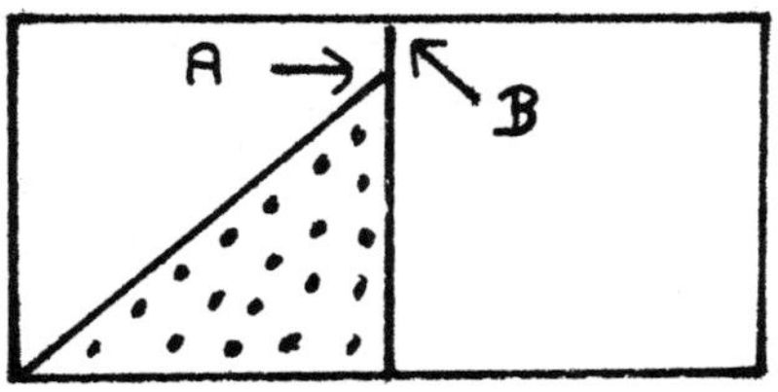

A →   ↖ B

join the rows together. Sew the three parts of row 2, and the three parts of row 3, again pressing all the seams. Now match center seams and join row 1 to row 2, and then add row 3. Make all the seams as flat as possible. Press the finished square.

"QUILT IN"

The purpose of quilting is to hold the three layers together: the top, the batting, and the back (the back square is the underside of a quilt block, sometimes called the "backing" square). Stack, then baste the layers—the backing, batting, and top square—together like a sandwich. Baste the square with the knots on top for easy removal (*Figure 72*).

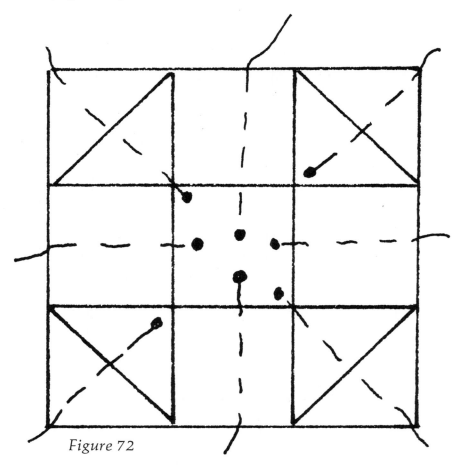

Figure 72

How to Quilt

The quilting stitch is a small running stitch going down through all three layers: the top, the batting, and the backing. It is evenly spaced and evenly stitched. Generally, you should have five to seven stitches to the inch, but don't worry if you don't—you should improve with practice (*Figures 73, 74*).

Figure 73 Quilting Stitch

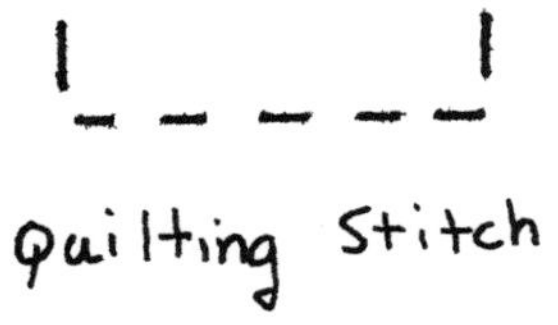

Figure 74 running stitch

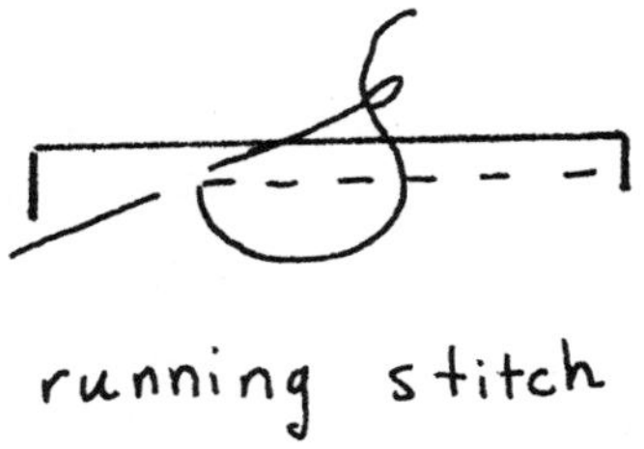

Thread a needle with a single piece of quilting thread. Make a *small* knot, snip off the tail, and put your thimble on the third finger of your hand. Start by coming up from underneath at the center-most point (*Figure 75*). Give a quick pull, losing the knot in the batting—it makes a clicking sound. (This may take some practice. Pulling the backing square away makes it easier for the knot to slip through.) Go straight down through all three layers, touching your

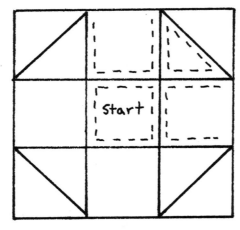

Figure 75

finger, and then come up to the top, making a small stitch. (Touching your finger ensures that you have gone through the three layers.) Take two, three, or four stitches on the needle and then draw through. If your finger gets sore wrap a piece of adhesive tape around it. This helps!

To end the thread off, go down to the underside of the backing square and take a stitch, going through the backing square and catching some batting. Then take another stitch right over the previous stitch. Now run the needle off to the side through the batting, pull the fabric up a little, and snip the thread off. The end is lost between the layers.

The amount of quilting you do is a matter of personal preference. It is most important to quilt from the center of the square toward the edges. This prevents the batting from bunching up in the center. Don't pull the stitches too tightly; let them flow. A very *important* point to remember: don't quilt any closer to the edge of the square than a good ½ inch. You will need the ½ inch of unquilted fabric when you join the square to another square in sewing the quilt together. (More than ½ inch unquilted fabric around the edge makes the whole process even easier!)

"Rome wasn't built in a day"—one square leads to another! Finish all the squares and turn to Chapter 4, "Building Blocks into Quilts," and put it together.

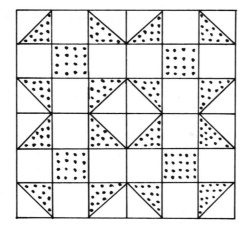

4
BUILDING BLOCKS INTO QUILTS

The squares are finished—
hurray, you did it!

Join all the squares together.

Lay the squares on the floor in their proper place. Sew all of row 1 together as follows (*Figure 76*): Starting with squares 1 and 2, place right sides together and sew a seam joining just the tops, not the batting or backing. Use a running stitch or sewing machine and

Figure 76

allow at least ¼-inch seam allowance. Sew all the squares together in each row, and then lay each row down on the floor in proper order (*Figure 77*).

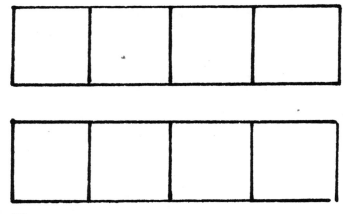

Figure 77

Working with each row *wrong* side up:

1. Place seam allowance (the top square seams you have just sewn) to one side—do not open seam.

2. Place batting from one side over the seam.

3. Trim batting from the other side so it abuts.

4. Lay backing from one side over batting, trimming when necessary.

5. The backing from the other side is turned under ¼ inch and placed over the previous seam. This seam is folded and pinned in the same direction on all the blocks. Do not sew yet—only pin (*Figure 78*)!

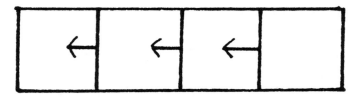

Figure 78

THE END IS IN SIGHT—JOIN THE ROWS

Starting with the first row: Right sides together, match the center seams, pinning and stitching just the tops, not the batting or the backing. Use a running stitch or machine and allow at least ¼-inch seam allowance. Continue joining all the horizontal rows in this manner (*Figure 79*).

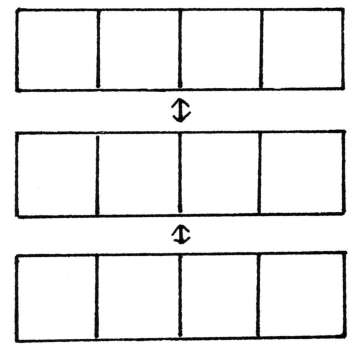

Figure 79

Turn the quilt over so the back is facing up. The vertical rows are neatly pinned. Begin with the first horizontal row and place the seam allowance (of the seams you have just sewn) to one side. Do not open the seams. Place the batting from one side over the seam, and trim the batting from the other side as it abuts. Then lay the backing over the batting and trim when necessary. Adjust all the vertical seams so they match up with all the other vertical seams in all the rows.

The mystery of the extra ½-inch larger back square unravels: you need it to help all the seams match up.

All the vertical seams are facing in the same direction. Now pin the horizontal seams in the same direction (*Figure 80*).

Blind stitch all the back seams of the quilt.

Hang in there—the quilt is almost finished. All it needs is framing. Now on to the edges.

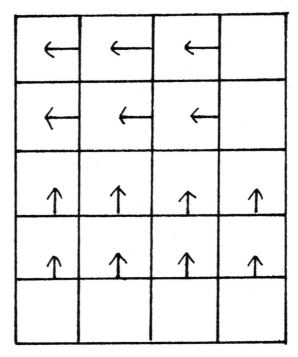

Figure 80

STRIPS AND BORDERS

Trim all four edges of your quilt so they are even. Strips and borders are attached to the quilt in the same manner. Strips are narrow and do not need batting. Borders are wide and therefore must have batting and should be quilted.

Strips

First, pin the *width* strips, right sides together, to the top and bottom of the quilt. Stitch by hand or machine through all thick-

nesses. Fold the strips over the ends of the quilt and turn the raw
edge under ¼ inch. Blind stitch to the quilt back, being sure to cover
the previous seam. Trim the excess strip even with the sides of the
quilt (*Figure 81*).

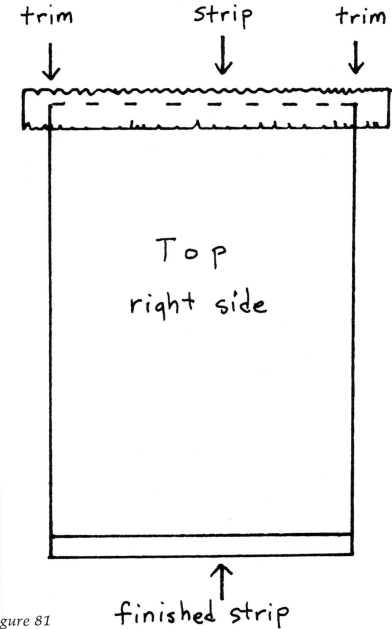

Figure 81

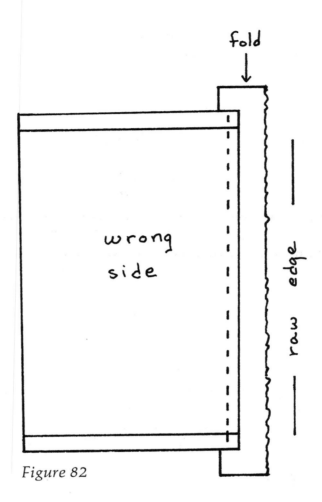

Figure 82

With right sides together, pin the *length* strips to both sides of the quilt, allowing the extra inches to hang over both ends. Stitch by hand or machine through all thicknesses. Turn the quilt over, fold the extra inches to the back, and pin (*Figure 82*). Turn the outside raw edge under ¼ inch, fold the strip over, and blind stitch to the quilt back, covering the previous seam.

Borders

Fold borders in half lengthwise and press, making a sharp crease. Cut the batting as follows: Take one width border and cut a piece of batting the same size. Now cut the batting in half lengthwise, making the two pieces needed for the top and bottom borders. Cut the batting for the *length* the same way but make it longer to include the width of the finished top and bottom borders.

Pin the width borders on both ends of the quilt, right sides together. Stitch by hand or machine through all thicknesses. Turn the quilt over so that the wrong side of the quilt and borders are facing up. Lay the batting between the quilt edge and the crease (*Figure 83*). Fold the border over the batting so the crease becomes the outside edge of the quilt. Turn the raw edge under, being sure that your seam is covered, and pin carefully. Baste the border across its width to secure the batting *before* you blind stitch it down to the back of the quilt.

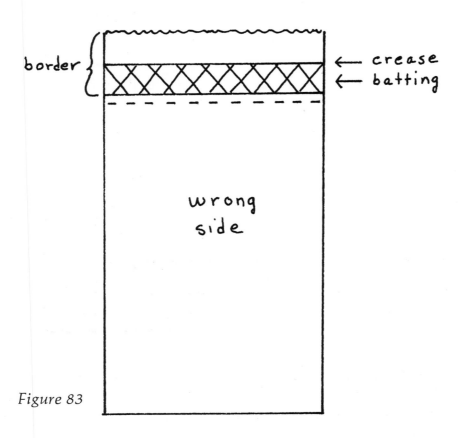

Figure 83

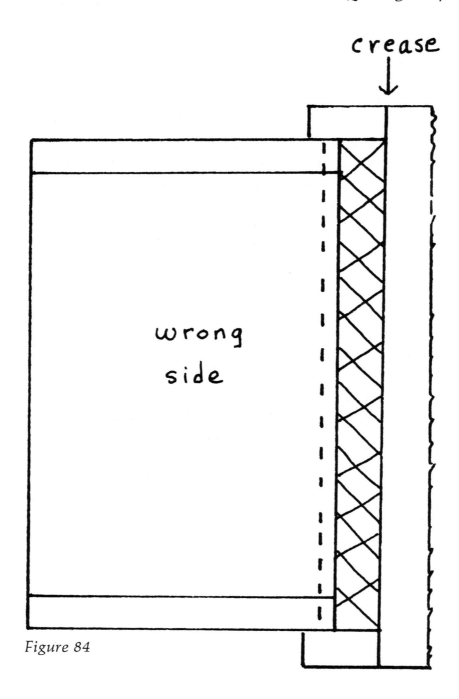

Figure 84

Pin the length borders on the quilt with right sides together, allowing the extra inches to hang over the finished top and bottom borders. Stitch by hand or machine through all thicknesses. Turn the quilt over so that the wrong side of the quilt and border is facing up. Lay the batting between the quilt edge and the crease, trimming if necessary (*Figure 84*).

Fold the border over the batting so the crease becomes the outside edge of the quilt. Turn the raw edge under, being sure that your seam is covered, and pin carefully. Baste the border across the width to secure the batting *before* you blind stitch it down to the back of the quilt.

FAMILY REJOICES

The heirloom quilt is finished. Beds will now be made, laundry will be done, and dinner will be on time! Proudly embroider your name and date on the back.

YOU HAVE MADE A QUILT!

See Plate 21.

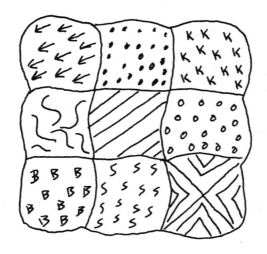

5
FURTHER FUN

Tie One On

A tied quilt is a quick quilt and a confidence-builder. It is made by joining all the top squares together, making the whole quilt top in one piece (*Figure 85*). The batting and the backing are each bought in one large piece. A sheet could be used for the backing. Batting can be bought in all sizes except king size. When making a king-size tied

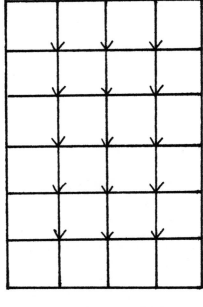

Figure 85

Tied Quilt

quilt buy two packages of single-bed size and join them together with long basting stitches (*Figure 86*). See Plate 9.

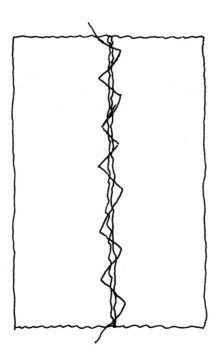

Figure 86

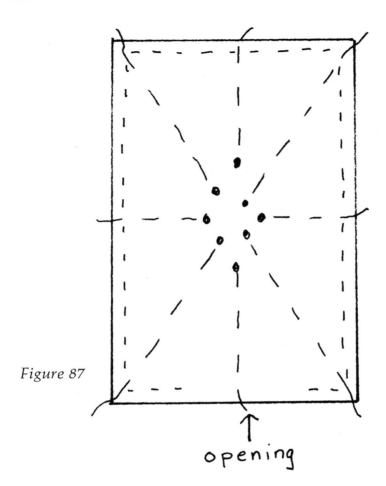

Figure 87

opening

Place the tied quilt on the floor in the following order:

1. The batting.

2. The backing with the *right* side facing up.

3. The quilt top with the *wrong* side facing up.

Pin and baste the layers together, working from the center out to the edges. Stitch on the machine (or by hand) around the edges, being sure to catch all three layers (*Figure 87*). Leave one end open for turning. Trim the edges even if necessary. Turn the quilt inside out and blind stitch the opening closed.

Tie It

Place the quilt on the floor with the side you want the knots to be on facing up. Mark with pins where knots will go (*Figure 88*). Thread a needle with yarn. Go down through the three layers, take a ¼-inch stitch on the underneath side, and come back up to the top. Make a square knot. (For the benefit of the non-yachting sewer here's how: right over left tie, and then left over right tie.) Snip the ends off to the length you want.

CRAZY THINGS WITH "CRAZY PATCH"

Cut a 12-inch square of muslin. Start at one corner and pin scraps of different colors and prints on top of the muslin base. Overlap them as you pin. Arrange and rearrange—do your thing. Turn the edges under ¼ inch and blind stitch down. On the underneath

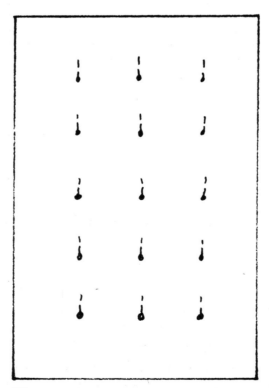

Figure 88

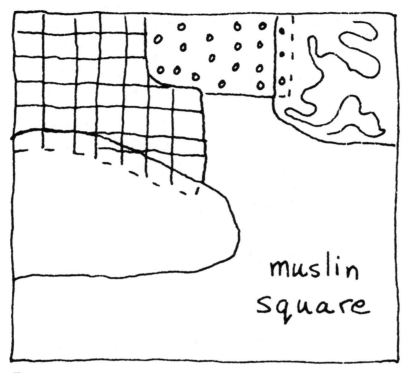

Figure 89

pieces leave the raw edges flat when possible. Cut away excess material to reduce the bulk (*Figure 89*).

"Crazy Patch" can be made on the sewing machine, using the zigzag stitch. Raw edges are left lying flat and are zigzagged over.

Press the square when it is completed.

The seams may be covered with embroidery stitches. This adds to the beauty of a crazy quilt.

Don't quilt "Crazy Patch." There are too many thicknesses, so tie it. One way to tie it is to have the ties show only on the back because very often the top is busy enough. Starting at the center of the square, bring the ties from the back up toward the top, but catch only the muslin base. Then go down through the back and make a square knot. It is a little easier, however, to come all the way through to the top, make a small stitch, and go back down with a square knot on the back.

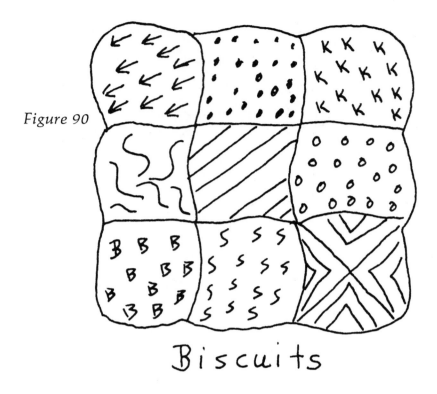

Figure 90

Biscuits

BISCUITS

Biscuits are puffy squares filled with pillow stuffing instead of batting. They are whipped together to make a quilt (*Figure 90*). Biscuits may be any size. The top square is always 1½ inches larger than the bottom square. See Plate 12.

Cut two cardboard patterns, one large and one small. Use the large pattern on one fabric and the small on another. (The small pattern is for the bottom and the larger one for the top.)

Right sides together, pin at the corners one large square and one small square (*Figure 91*). Then pin a pleat on each side of all the corners. The pleats face the center (*Figure 92*). Stitch a ¼-inch seam around. Leave an opening on one side for turning inside out (*Figure 93*).

Turn inside out and stuff with pillow stuffing. Blind stitch the opening closed.

Make another biscuit. Join the two by placing the bottom sides together and whipping across the edge. This seam will not show.

Young people, especially boys, seem to love this type of quilt.

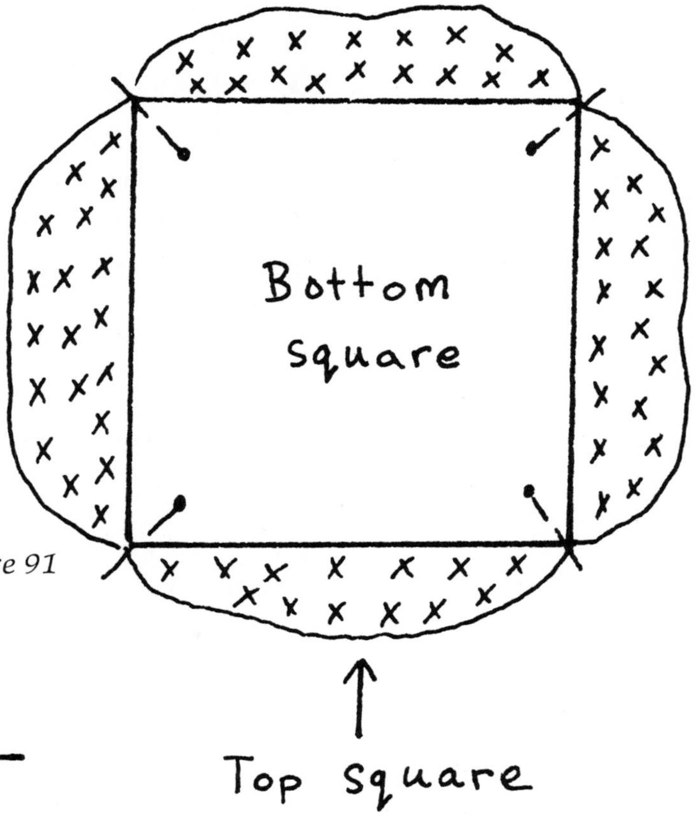

Figure 91

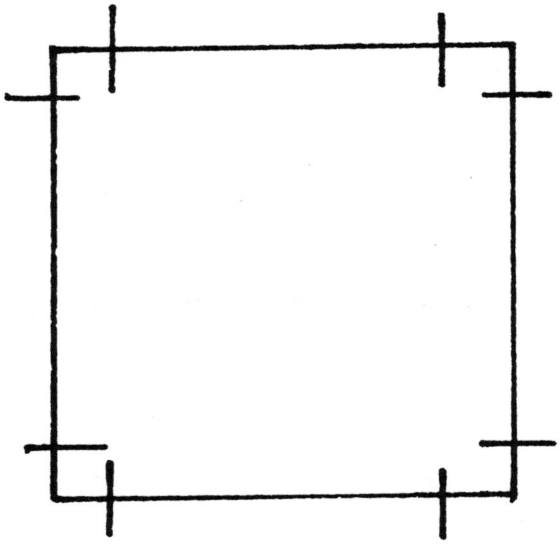

Bottom square

Top square

Figure 92

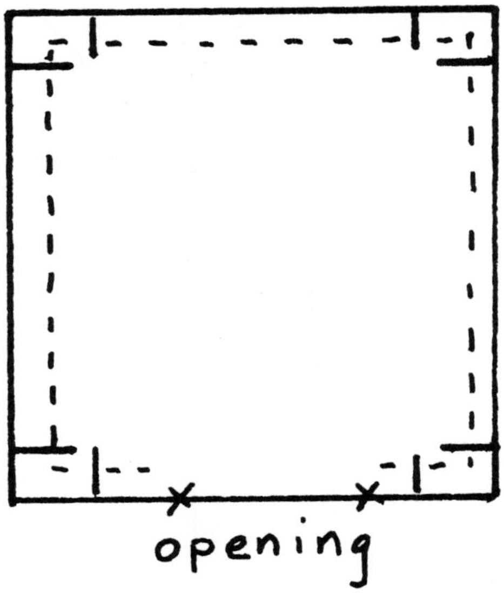

Figure 93

opening

"CATHEDRAL WINDOW"

"Cathedral Window" is very impressive and makes a lovely pillow or a beautiful coverlet. It is never quilted. When the fabric is sewn together the square is finished! See Plate 13.

Cut two accurate 9-inch squares of plain fabric. With right sides *inside*, fold each square in half and stitch a ¼-inch seam on each end (*Figure 94*). This sewing may be done by hand or machine.

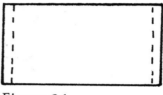

Figure 94

One at a time, make a square by matching center seams of line *A–B* (*Figure 95*). Sew by hand or machine seam *C–D*, leaving an opening for turning (*Figure 96*).

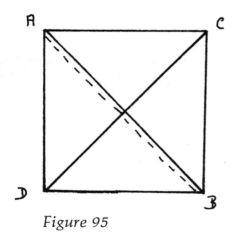

Figure 95

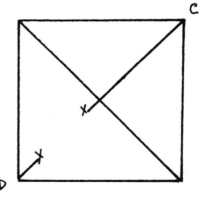

Figure 96

Turn each square right side out, poking the corners with a pencil so they are sharp. Blind stitch the opening closed. Press.

Place each square in front of you with the seam side down. Using a double thread, place the needle through the tip of point *A* in *Figure 97*. Don't worry about the knot on top showing. Then pick up point *B* the same way, drawing both together so the points touch each other, meeting at the center (*Figure 98*). Put the needle through

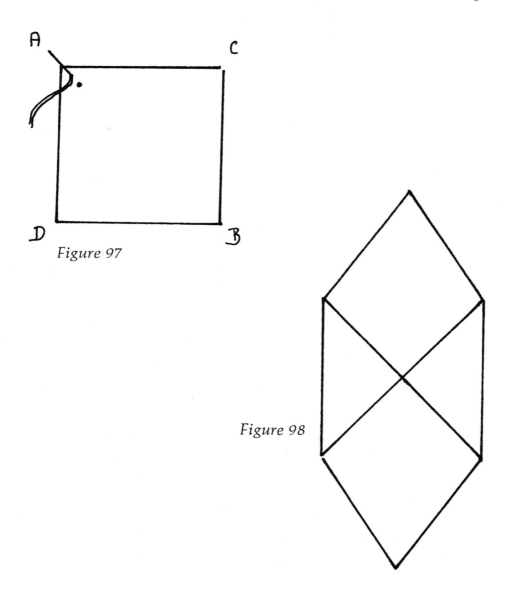

Figure 97

Figure 98

to the underside at the intersection, come back up to the top, and pick up points *C* and *D* as you did *A* and *B*. Go down through the intersection again and then come back up and knot the thread off. Press. The two squares will look like *Figures 99* and *100*.

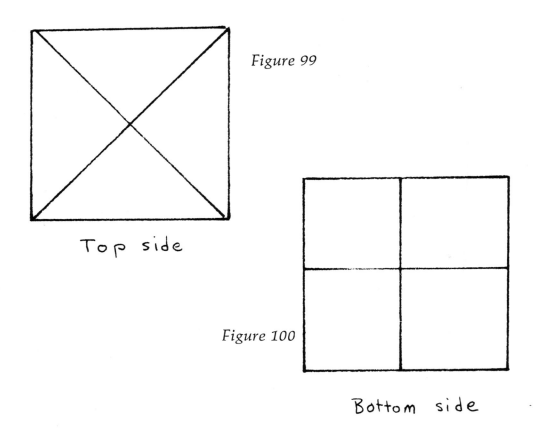

Figure 99

Top side

Figure 100

Bottom side

Join the two squares by placing the bottom sides together, matching the center seam, and whipping across the edge. This is the seam you will cover with a print fabric to make the "window" (*Figure 101*).

Cut a small print square ¼ inch *smaller* than the area you are covering. Pin it on top of the seam. Start in the middle of one side, turn the folded edge over the print fabric, and blind stitch it down. Sew all four sides (*Figure 102*).

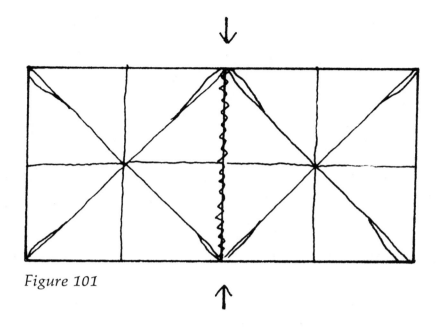

Figure 101

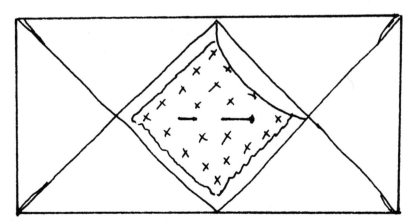

Figure 102

You need nine squares to make a pillow. Each row is made up of three squares. You must complete each row first and then whip the rows together. You will see that in joining the rows you will create a seam that must be covered with print fabric (*Figure 103*).

You may want to fold back the folds on the outside sections and blind stitch them down (line *A–B* in the figure). This gives the top a finished look and makes a pattern of the folded edges. A little piece of pillow stuffing can also be put under the small print fabric. This gives an added puffy look.

When you make a "Cathedral Window" pillow the cording is placed on the pillow back. The "Cathedral Window" top is then sewn on by hand.

You may join many blocks together (by rows—important!) to make a lovely coverlet.

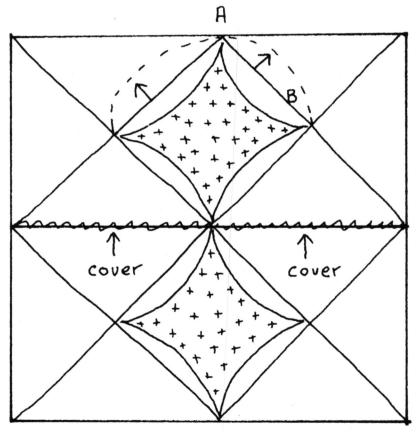

Figure 103

"GRANDMOTHER'S FLOWER GARDEN" PILLOW

Use two or three print fabrics and a plain color. The plain color is the path" running through "Grandmother's Garden." See Plate 14.

Make fabric hexagons, using the hexagon pattern (*Figure 104*). Then whip them together, following *Figure 105*:

1.   Whip all the hexagons in each row together.

2.   Then join the rows, fitting each hexagon into place. You will be sewing one side of the hexagon at a time, zigzagging as you sew.

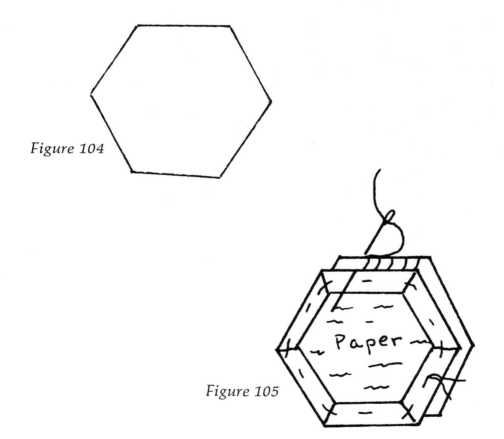

Figure 104

Figure 105

Press the hexagon flower and then remove the papers. Blind stitch it onto a background square. Press again and get it ready for quilting. Quilt it, stuff it, and present it to "Grandpa."

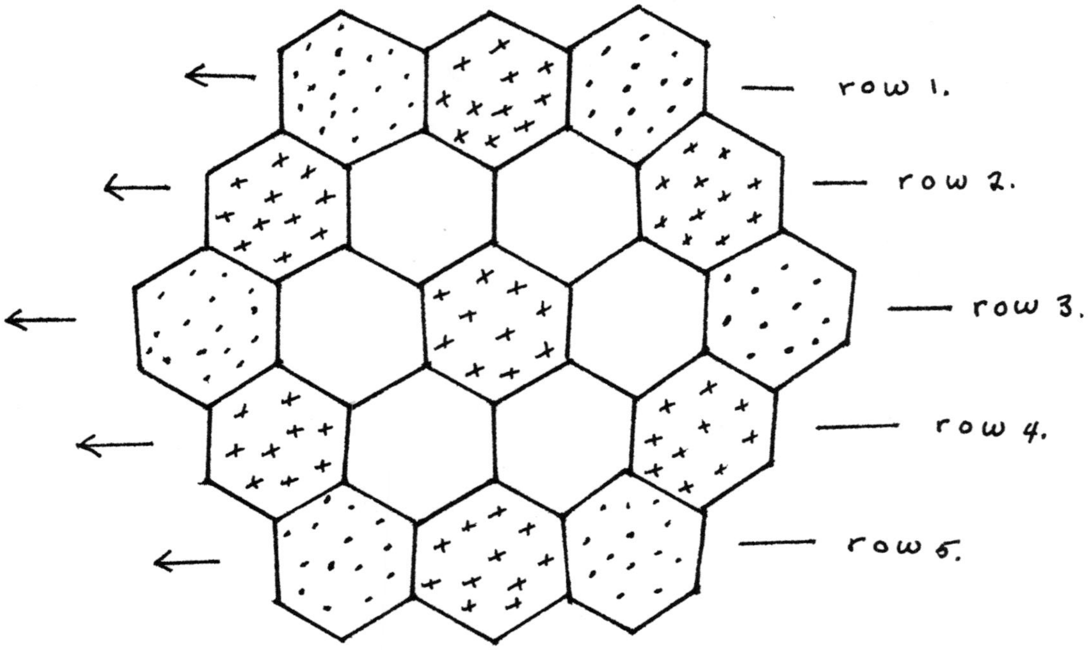

Figure 106

ADDITIONAL QUILT PATTERNS

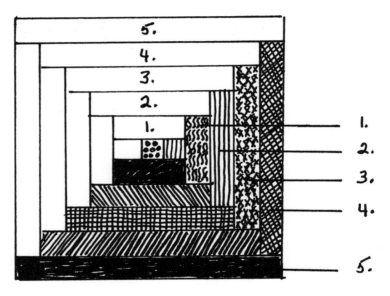

Log Cabin

See Plate 19.

LOG CABIN

This variation is called "Barn Raising."

Each square has a dark and a light side. Cut three center pieces 1½ inches by 1½ inches. All the rest of the strips are 1½ inches by:

1 = 3½ inches
2 = 5½ inches
3 = 7½ inches
4 = 9½ inches
5 = 11½ inches

Cut two lights and two darks of each size for one square with the exception of number 5, which has only one dark and one light.

First sew the three small center pieces together, then:

add number 1 light strip to the top
add number 1 dark strip to the bottom
add number 1 light strip to the side
add number 1 dark strip to the other side

Continue adding:

number 2 light strip to the top
number 2 dark strip to the bottom
number 2 light strip to the light side
number 2 dark strip to the dark side

It is very important to add the strips in this order. The last row has only one dark and one light strip. The seam allowance taken should be ¼ inch. It is included in the pattern. This square will measure approximately 11 inches.

WREATH OF ROSES APPLIQUÉ

The circle for the wreath is made from a bias strip. It is sewn in place first on a background square. The flowers and leaves are then placed on top and blind stitched down.

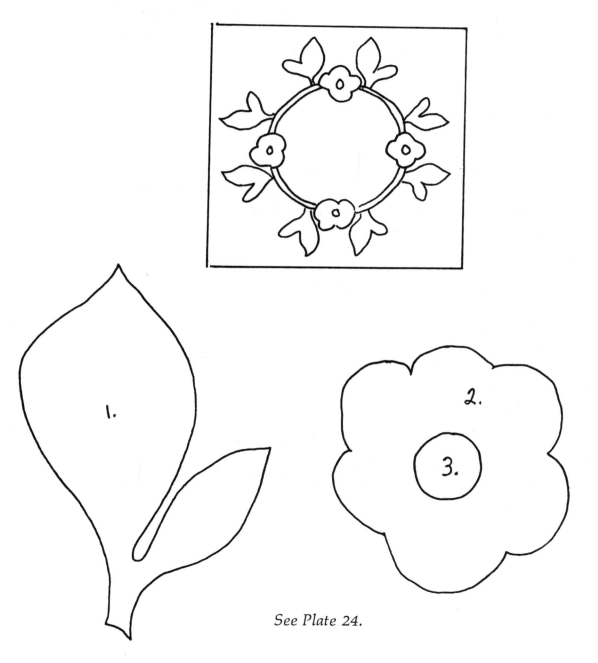

See Plate 24.

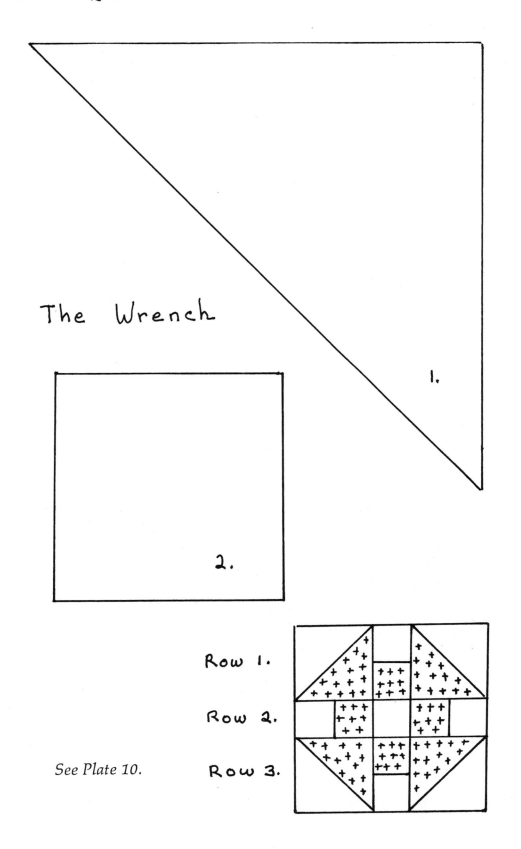

The Wrench

1.

2.

Row 1.

Row 2.

See Plate 10.

Row 3.

See Plate 21.

1.

2.

3.

Hen and Chicks Appliqué with Embroidery

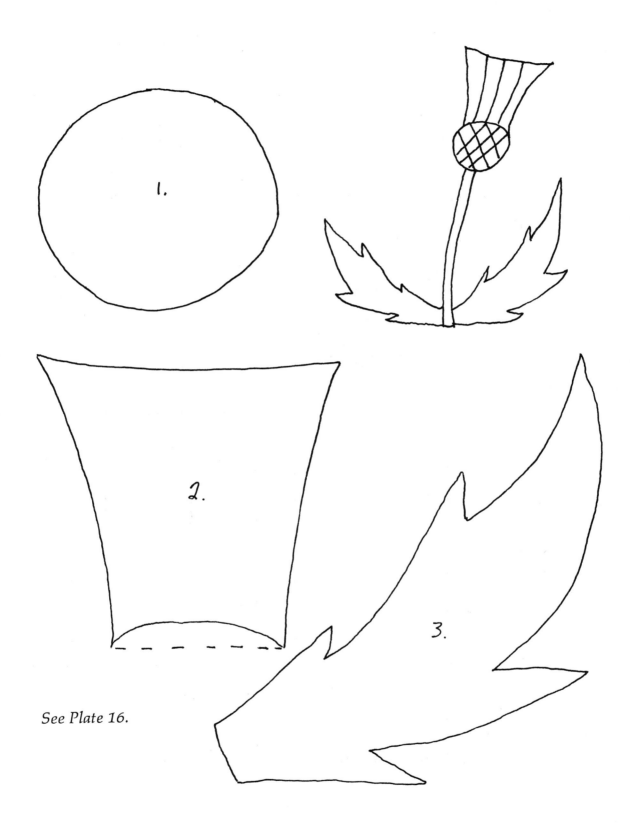

1.

2.

3.

See Plate 16.

Appliqué and Quilting

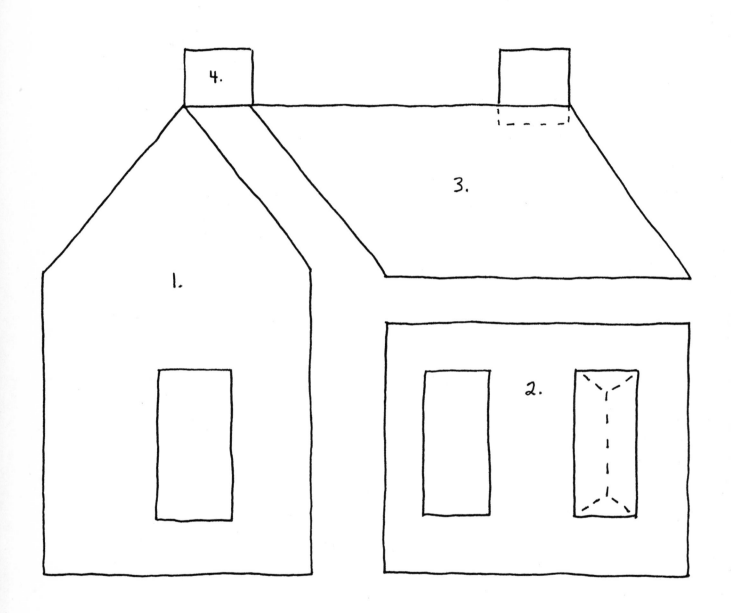

School House Appliqué

SCHOOL HOUSE APPLIQUÉ

Cut each section from colorful calico and appliqué the pieces in place on a background square.

Slit the windows as shown by the broken lines, fold the edges under, and blind stitch down. Add embroidery for the shutters.

You will need to add a ¼-inch seam allowance to each section.

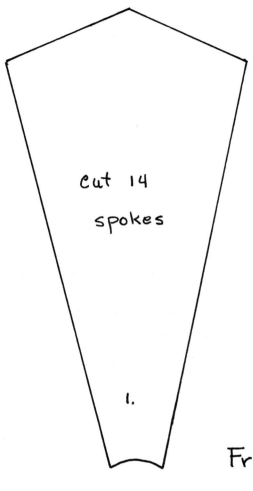

cut 14

spokes

1.

Friendship "Wheel"

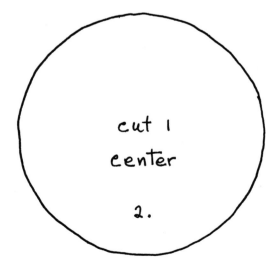

cut 1

center

2.

See Plate 17.

THE FRIENDSHIP "WHEEL"

Its proper name is "Friendship Ring" or "Dresden Plate."

The pattern is given without the seam allowance, but the best way to make it up is to include the seam allowance in the pattern. Work with two patterns as you do in piecework, two with the seam allowance and one without.

Seam the spokes together. Press and blind stitch down on a 14-inch background square. Appliqué the center on top.

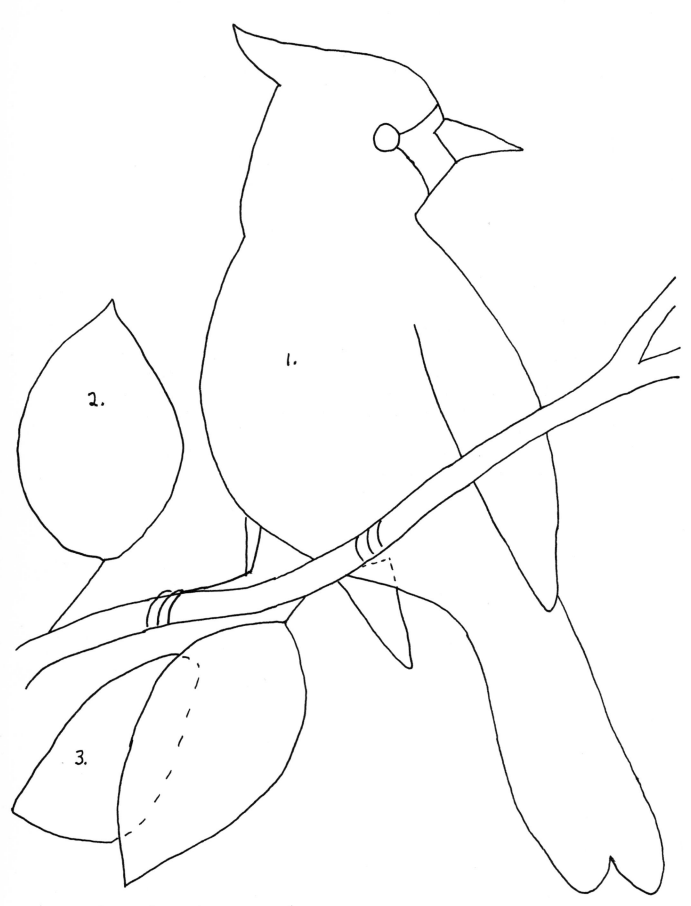

Cardinal Appliqué with Embroidery

A B C D E F
G H I J K L M
N O P Q R S T U
V W X Y Z

a b c d e f
g h i j k l m
n o p q r s t u
v w x y z

1 2 3 4 5 6 7 8 9 0

Barbara
November 28, 1955

Fold

Plain Quilting

Embroidered
Name and Date

Terms Used in Quilt-making

Appliqué—A free-form pattern "laid" on a top square.

Backing square—Underside of the quilt block.

Batting—The filler inside the quilt.

Block—One square in a quilt.

Patchwork—A combination of piecework and appliqué—for example, the piecing of geometrical shapes, appliquéd on a top square.

Piecework—Geometrical-shape pieces of fabric sewn together to make up a design.

Quilt—A bed covering made up of two pieces of cloth with a filler in between. Stitched designs hold the layers together. This is called quilting.

Selvage—An edge of a woven fabric, so formed as to prevent raveling.

Setting—The arrangement of all the squares, or blocks, in a quilt.

Straight of goods—There are two straights: one follows the vertical selvage and the other is at right angles to it (across the width of the fabric).

Template—A pattern used in quilt-making.

Top square—Top face of the quilt block.

Bibliography

Bogen, Constance. *A Beginners' Book of Patchwork, Appliqué and Quilting.* New York: Dodd, Mead and Company, 1974.

Frager, Dorothy. *The Quilting Primer.* Radnor, Pennsylvania: Chilton Book Company, 1974.

Heard, Audrey, and Pryor, Beverly. *Complete Guide to Quilting.* Des Moines, Iowa: Meredith Corp./Better Homes and Gardens, 1974.

Lehman, Bonnie. *Quick and Easy Quilting.* New York: Hearthside Press, 1972.

Mahler, Celine Blanchard. *Once Upon a Quilt.* New York: Van Nostrand Reinhold Co., 1973.

Wilson, Erica. *Crewel Embroidery.* New York: Charles Scribner's Sons, 1962.